BENEATH GREEN SHADOWS

by

Maurice Stanley

BENEATH GREEN SHADOWS

by
Maurice Stanley

11 Let the heavens rejoice, and let the earth be glad;
let the sea roar, and the fulness thereof.
12 Let the field be joyful, and all that *is* therein: then
shall all the trees of the wood rejoice.

- Psalm 96:11-12

ISBN: 149609218X
ISBN 13: 9781496092182
Library of Congress Control Number: 2014904073
CreateSpace Independent Publishing Platform
North Charleston, South Carolina

DEDICATION

To my brother Stephen

CONTENTS

PREFACE

Waterville, North Carolina is located in Haywood County near the North Carolina-Tennessee state line.

Alice and Ansel Harper and their small son, Jody, lived in the little village which was built to house the families of those who worked at the Walters Hydroelectric power plant. The little village also had a post office, a school, a boarding house, and a club house. It was a beautiful place, with woods all around and a river nearby. The plant, an imposing structure of brick with tall windows, was built during 1927-1930. When Ansel Harper worked at the plant it was owned by Carolina Power and Light Company.

Waterville in 1950 was a peaceful, idyllic place, and the Harper family, like the other families in the village, were mostly content and civilized, and the age-old forest that enfolded it gave it the character of a green, quiet paradise. Even now it looks like a picture from the cover of a book of fairy tales.

But even beautiful paradises and enchanted fairy-tale kingdoms often hide things cruel and evil. In Waterville, in 1950, this evil being was named "Willis Broom."

Waterville Power Plant

Waterville Power Plant
Shows the tailrace

Ansel and Alice Harper

The Waterville House – Ansel Harper in the yard 1970

The Waterville House –
Alice Harper sitting by the river 1970

Alice Harper and Jody Harper

Alice Harper and Jody Harper
In front of Tennessee Sign

Jody Harper and
Ansel Harper

Jody Harper

Jody Harper Inside the Car

Jody Harper in his Gene Autry outfit

Mt. Sterling School

Maurice Stanley, the author, and his wife, Glana – 1970

Mt. Sterling Schoolhouse

June 2010

Willis Broom and Carolyn Broom

Drawings by Maurice Stanley, the author

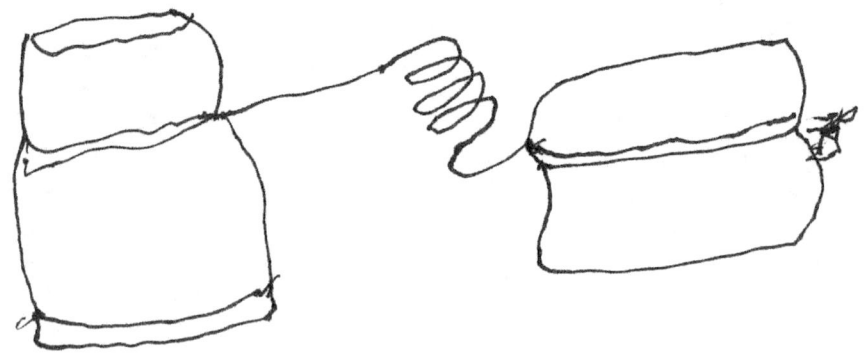

Willis Broom's whiskey still

Drawing by Maurice Stanley, the author

Pete Broom, the Sheriff

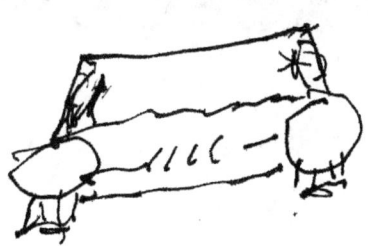

Pete Broom's Car

Drawing by Maurice Stanley, the author

Alice Harper and Ansel Harper
50th Wedding Anniversary
August 1992

Shoe Store

After Ansel Harper retired from Carolina Power and Light Company, he built a shoe store and had the business for 30 years.

CHAPTER ONE

The night air was cool as Ansel Harper left the plant. As he walked along the iron platform that led from the door of the plant to the parking lot he looked down into the tailrace, dark and churning. He thought once more about the miracle of electricity.

Preachers often explained God by reference to electricity. We don't understand electricity, and yet the light burns, they said. The same with God. We don't understand God, but His work shines all around us, they would say. Ansel didn't accept that. Electricity could be understood.

Ansel mused that at least he understood how the light bulbs came to shine, even if the preachers did not. And besides, he thought, if nobody understood it how the hell could we ever have got electricity? How could they ever have built this great power plant?

He looked back at the plant, a huge, rectangular brick building set into the mountain. It stood in the moonlight like the door to a gargantuan castle. It was as if you could open it up and see deep into the secret places of Earth.

Ansel carried his lunch box and a quart Mason jar for the jarfly he had promised Jody. He walked in the dark toward the end of the swinging bridge. Suddenly he sensed something before him in the dark. He stopped.

Out of the shadows came a familiar figure. In the light Ansel could see his huge frame looming before him. "What do you want with me, Willis?" Ansel asked.

"This is what I want with you, Harper," Willis said, and hit Ansel full in the face. Ansel went down, dropping his lunch box and the Mason jar. The Mason jar shattered.

Ansel lay looking up at Willis. In the lamplight he could see the outline of a pistol against the sweaty white shirt. He stayed down.

"That's for getting me fired, you son-of-a-bitch," Willis said, stepping over him and walking toward the road that led to Newport. "And I'm not through with you yet, you sneaking bastard. I'll kill you, but not tonight."

Ansel picked himself up when Willis had left and dusted his pants off. In the dark he heard a cicada and he looked for it and caught it. He put it into his lunch box. His thermos rattled, so he knew it was broken. He went toward the bridge. His jaw hurt and felt gritty.

From the porch Jody could see the river in the moonlight. Through the tall pines along the sidewalk he was watching the far end of the swinging bridge that went from the settlement to the plant across the river. His father would appear under the street lamp with his lunchbox, walk across the bridge and up the sidewalk through the shadows beside the river and then up the hundred steps up the steep bank to the house.

"What time is it, Mommy?" he shouted through the window.

"Shh, son, you mustn't holler out like that. The neighbors are asleep. It's nearly twelve. He'll be home pretty soon." I'll be glad when he gets off the evening shift, she mumbled to herself as she put the coffee pot on the stove.

It was wise to stay on good terms with the neighbors. Sometimes a job could depend on it, and no time, not even 1950, was a good time to be out of work.

Jody watched and waited. He could smell the woods around the house, utterly dark and cool, high above where the street lamps shone. The woods were not frightening to him. They were part of his world, part of him. He could feel them. It was dark on the porch. He had cut the yellow porch light off so he could see across the river.

All around the house the night lay, friendly and hospitable.

Jody was waiting up for his father to bring him a jarfly – a huge cicada that came out in the cool summer nights.

"What time is it now, Mommy?" he asked through the screen door.

"It's about twelve fifteen. He should be home by now. He's late. Maybe Turner went in late tonight and Ansel's had to work overtime." She was not worried. He had been late before. Like the time Jamison had had his heart attack. Ansel had to work overtime that time, about four hours' worth.

The front porch swing squeaked loudly as Jody swung back and forth. He could see the two cedar trees at the end of the sidewalk and he could see down the steps to the sidewalk, at the bottom of the steps, that led to the swinging bridge. When his father first appeared Jody would see him coming in and out of the shadows the street lamps made of the trees along the walk. And he would have a jarfly, like he promised. Ansel never broke a promise to him.

"He won't forget, son. But if he does, I don't want you to cry. You're too big to cry."

Alice turned on the radio. The only station on that late at night was WCKY, Cincinnati. It played country music all night long. A song by Lefty Frizzell was playing. She began to worry a little. Why was Ansel so late? It was nearly twelve-thirty. Sure enough, the twelve-thirty newscast was coming on, with John Cameron Swaze, about Truman and the Cold War with Russia. The Second World War had been over for five years and things were pretty good.

Alice wished he didn't have to work shift work. The evening shift was hard. The graveyard shift was easy, but it ruined Ansel's sleeping habits. The day shift was best. Most of the storms happened on the evening shift, and that was hard work for the dispatcher on duty.

Alice turned the porch light on and went out and sat down with Jody on the porch swing. They swung back and forth, back and forth, and waited, watching the swinging bridge.

Ansel walked across the swinging bridge with tears in his eyes. He should have fought back, maybe, but Willis had been carrying a gun. It would have been suicidal to try to fight Willis.

Alice and Jody could see him coming across the bridge. Then, as he came up the sidewalk they could see him coming in and out of the light. His shadow would start out small and grow larger and larger before him and then it would fade and disappear and a new one would start behind him. Jody held his breath until he could hear his daddy's footsteps. Then click, click, click, up the hundred steps to the sidewalk where the two cedars were and now Alice and Jody could see him quite well.

Alice could see the blood on Ansel's face from the porch light. And there was blood on his shirt sleeve where he had scraped his elbow when he fell.

"What on earth, Ansel?" she shouted.

"Sh, sh," Ansel said. "Let's go in the house."

"What happened?" she asked again when they were inside.

"First," he said, "I've got something for Jody. Look here, son." He opened his lunch box and the jarfly flew out.

Jody was delighted and ran around the house trying to catch it.

Then Ansel looked at Alice. Alice ran to the kitchen and brought back a wet rag to wipe the blood from Ansel's mouth.

"Willis Broom," Ansel said. "He caught me in the dark coming home. He knocked me down and called me a son-of-a-bitch. I didn't fight him. I couldn't, Alice. He was carrying that gun, that Smith and Wesson .38 revolver, in his belt. It was under his shirt, but I could see it."

"I'm glad you didn't fight him, Ansel," she said, kissing him on the head and petting him. "Jody and I couldn't do without you. I wish we could leave here and go somewhere civilized. It's too rough back in these woods. How long is Willis going to carry that grudge, anyway? It's been a year since they fired him."

"Willis will never forget it. He was coming in drunk on the job. He could have killed somebody, some lineman working on the power lines. I had to tell Mr. Calloway. I'm sorry I did it. I wish I hadn't. But Willis will never forget it."

"How does he make a living, now, Ansel?" Alice asked.

"He moonshines and Johnny Bryson runs the stuff into Asheville. Pete, the sheriff is Willis's brother, you know, and just as low and sneaking and mean as Willis. It wouldn't do any good to turn him in. It's a bad situation."

"Let's leave here, Ansel. Let's go back over the mountain to Asheville."

"I can't run, Sweetheart. You know that. He'd come over the mountains after me. We'd have to move to Timbucktu. And besides, I've got a good job here. Jobs are hard to find. You don't want to go back on welfare, do you?"

"No," she sighed. "But I wish we could get away from here. Why don't you put in for a transfer, Honey? There's plenty of other places where the power company has substations."

"Maybe I will. But I'm afraid I'll have to settle with Willis before I go."

"You'd have to kill him, or him you, to settle it," Alice said.

Jody had caught the jarfly and he brought it to them. "Give me a jar, Mommy," he said.

"Okay, son," she said, "just a minute." She went to the kitchen and got another Mason jar.

Jody put the bug in the jar and clapped the lid on it. Then he saw his father's face. "What's the matter with your face, Daddy?" he asked.

"Nothing, son. I fell. That's all. And it's your bedtime, Buddro. Give me and Mommy a kiss and get off to bed."

Jody went to bed. Ansel and Alice sat down at the kitchen table to have their one last cup of coffee before bed.

"Did you have an easy shift, Honey?" Alice asked.

"Yes, it was all right. Some storms are expected this weekend, though. Summer storms kick up quite a lot of power problems, sometimes. I'll be on evening shift 'til Monday. Then I'm off two days and then I go in on days for awhile."

"I wish you could get on day shift all the time. This shift work is killing us both."

"Jody will start to school this Fall, won't he?" Ansel said.

"Yes. He'll have to go to Mt. Sterling School, that little one-room school-house a few miles up that dirt road up Cataloochee Mountain. He'll have to go to school with those filthy little Scoggins kids. And most of the people who live up that way are so poor. Ansel, I hate for him to have to go to school there. And Thelma Milsaps teaches up there, and so does Wilma Rogers. And you know how Wilma must feel about us, ever since last summer."

5

"Yes, I know."

He remembered last summer very well. Bob Rogers had come over to the house while Ansel was at work on day shift. He got up close to Alice and untied her apron strings. Alice didn't say anything about it, that time. But then the very next day he did it again, and that time he tried to kiss her, too. That time she told Ansel when he got in from work, and the next day Ansel went three houses down, to the Rogers house. He called Bob Rogers out in his yard and told him to stop bothering his wife, or, as Ansel said, he would "beat the living hell out of him." Then Ansel walked back home and pretty much forgot about it. It never happened again. But Wilma Rogers had been home, looking out the front window. Ansel saw her. She heard everything.

Some people never forgive anything, and Wilma Rogers would never forgive Ansel or Alice for the embarrassment that day had brought. She surely would take it out on Jody, because, despite the fact that she had a year of college, she was a fundamentally stupid woman.

"That's where he'll have to go to school, if we stay here," Ansel said.

"I hate it for Jody. This is such a <u>little</u> place, Ansel. The people here all know everybody else's business."

"That's not such a bad thing, Alice. It keeps people moral."

"Not people like Willis Broom," Alice said.

Jody was in bed but he was not asleep. He was thinking of his Daddy's face -- his red eyes and swollen jaw and the blood. From the bedroom he could hear them talking in the kitchen. He knew something was wrong but he didn't know what. After a while he went to sleep.

Late in the night Jody woke up and saw a faint light in the living room. He sneaked out of bed to look and it was his daddy, sitting up in the dark, in the big rocker, smoking a cigarette. And worrying, Jody knew, about Willis Broom.

* * *

The moon, almost full, hovered over the dark green trees of the woods all around Waterville. The little village lights sparkled in the midst of a dark ocean of shadows like the lights of a cruise ship in the night on the black sea.

The ancient Greeks and Romans had stories, myths, about trees. They believed that the forests were where the souls of people found their final resting places. The forests were peaceful and holy, and they were also places of celebration and the joys of love and wine. And the people of little Waterville Village, enfolded by the great, green forests of the Smoky Mountains, also found peace and pleasure in the quiet of the surrounding woods.

CHAPTER TWO

Newport, Tennessee was a rough little mountain town, and Willis Broom prided himself on being the roughest customer around. Rumor had it that he carried a .38 Smith and Wesson revolver under his shirt, and rumor was right.

He walked back to his truck from where he had left Ansel. What a lousy goddamn coward, Willis thought. I wish he'd fought back. I'd have shot him full of goddamn holes. Sooner or later I'll get him, he thought. I'll kill him. He had no cause but being Cal's goody-goody boy for telling Calloway about me drinking. I'll fix his ass so he won't tell on anybody else.

Willis had come in drunk on every shift for a month, so Ansel had told Calloway, and Calloway came to the plant in the middle of Willis' evening shift, caught Willis drunk and drinking on the job and fired him on the spot.

Willis had raged at Calloway and had finally hit him. Calloway was a frail middle-aged man, and Willis was huge and brawny -- six feet two inches, two hundred and forty pounds of fat and muscle. Willis broke Calloway's jaw and put him in the hospital for a week. Willis was ordered to stay away from the plant. No charges were brought.

Willis had a high-pitched, woman's voice. It was the memorable thing about him, besides his size. Both Willis and Pete had faces that could only be called dumb and mean. Pete lived a fairly upright sort of life, since he was sheriff. But Willis was always in trouble.

Willis thought about his latest trouble as he got into his old Chevrolet truck. Not Ansel. Ansel was no trouble. Sooner or later he would get Ansel for good. He was sure about that. No, his latest trouble was in Newport. There his brother Pete had no clout, and trouble across the state line was therefore real trouble. Pete was sheriff in Haywood County. But over in Tennessee Pete was nobody and could not help Willis. "Stay in Haywood County, Willis." That's what Pete was always telling him.

Willis was worried as he drove down the dark two-lane blacktop toward home. He was worried about what had happened the night before in Newport.

Willis had been drinking at the Hot Spot with some buddies, Jeff Spence and Ray Moore, and they began to talk about how easy it would be to rob a store. Which store? one asked. How about a service station? another said. Then they decided on the Texaco station outside town on 19 East. Willis said no, they might get caught.

"Chicken shit," one said.

"Yaller-belly!" the other said.

"Let's do it, then," Willis said.

"We'll wait 'til closing time," Ray said, "and we'll go in with that .38 you got under your shirt."

"Okay," Willis said, and so they got into his truck and headed out to the Texaco station. They parked in the shadows and waited for the attendant to close up. Sure enough, about nine o'clock the man in the station turned the lights off and walked out toward his car with a bag of money, the station's earnings for the day.

"Hold it," Ray said, jumping out of the truck.

"Hold it right there," Jeff repeated.

Willis drew his pistol and pointed it at the attendant. "Give us that money," he said.

The man gave Willis the money. "Please don't shoot me, buddy," the man said.

"Turn around," Willis said, and the man turned around, shaking.

Willis took aim at him and was about to shoot him when Ray and Jeff grabbed Willis.

"No! No!" Ray said, holding Willis's arm.

Willis took his finger off the trigger and slammed the gun down on the station attendant's head. "You'd better forget us," Willis said, "or we'll come back here and kill you deader'n hell."

So they left. Now Willis was worried. What if that guy told the police anyway? He ought to have shut him up for good. But then Ray and Jeff might have told on him. God, life was complicated. They got nearly five hundred dollars from the guy. His boss might ask him what happened to all the money. Would he tell? Well, hell, you can't worry about everything, Willis thought.

Willis drove toward his house in Red Dog, a little town -- a wide place in the road, really -- on the North Carolina side near Newport, Tennessee. His house was almost on the state line. The road was winding and curvy. A brighter soul than Willis might have called it circuitous. But Willis didn't know such words. There were many concepts which were too hard for Willis to grasp. But Willis understood getting even and not getting caught.

So Willis went down the dark highway in his truck, thinking his own dark, angry thoughts. Some of us are winners and some are losers, and I'm no loser. Ansel Harper, there's a loser. And old man Cal. Hee, hee, Willis laughed to himself, I busted that old bastard's face up good. And Ansel's, too. All around the night lay dark and still. Soon Willis would be home.

The house was dark and quiet when he pulled up in the dirt driveway. His wife, Carolyn, was in bed. He got out of the truck and walked the short distance to the house. He had a hard time finding the keyhole in the front door. He swore loudly and finally got the door open.

"Wake up, bitch!" he shouted as he slammed the door behind him. "Come on! Get up!"

Carolyn came out of the bedroom, rubbing her eyes. "Why can't you stay up and wait for me?" Willis stormed out.

"What?" Carolyn said, but Willis slapped her and she fell down. Blood came out her nose. Willis hit her again as she was getting up, knocking her down again.

"Don't, Willis, please," Carolyn cried.

She was still crying softly when he went to sleep.

The next morning Willis woke up to the smell of bacon and eggs frying. He pulled on his pants and went to the kitchen. Carolyn was just putting the eggs into the plate. She poured Willis some coffee and put the cream and sugar into it. He took it and sucked it noisily into his mouth.

Willis noticed that Carolyn had a black eye. He realized he'd been a little rough on her the night before. But hell, what's a woman for? He reached out and grabbed her between the legs, laughing.

"You love your ole mean Willis, Baby? Huh?"

She turned away from him. "You were drunk. I wish you wouldn't come in drunk, Willis. You're mean and you're big."

"That's me," Willis said. "Big and mean, mean and big."

After breakfast Willis went out in the woods to the clearing where he had his still under a big maple tree. Five dollars a pint in Asheville for moonshine was pretty good money. A whole case of twenty-four pint Mason jars of moonshine brought one hundred and twenty dollars. Two cases brought two hundred and forty dollars. Willis enjoyed that arithmetic, even though he had quit school in the fourth grade to help work around the family farm. His father had lost most of the farm through drinking and gambling a few years after. Not much was left to them but welfare and moonshine.

He lifted the bag of sugar on the back porch and brought it out to the still and poured it into the vat. Then he brought the corn and poured it in. Then he brought several buckets of water from the spring. He brought wood and put it under the vat and then lit it. After a while the mixture was bubbling. He stirred it a bit and capped the lid back on. Soon drops of moisture began to collect in the coils of the old car radiator and dripped in the collection vat. He would run off twelve or so pints before noon.

He grew his own corn and he bought the sugar at the general store in Newport. The people at the store in Newport were no more suspicious of Willis than they were of anybody else who bought lots of sugar. Lots of people did it. Lots of people moonshined.

Willis figured he would send two cases to Asheville that weekend. He would send it by Johnny Bryson. Johnny had a fast '49 Ford and had never been caught, and he'd been transporting moonshine for ten years. He would have to pay Johnny a little money for that, but Johnny loved running moonshine so much he'd almost do it for nothing.

Willis walked back toward the house and he was surprised to find Ray Moore parked in the yard in his old '46 Chevrolet.

"What you say, Willis?" Ray said, grinning.

"What you need?" Willis asked. He figured Ray was up to no good. He didn't like Ray coming to his house. They were drinking buddies, that was all.

"The police brought me in to question me about that robbery," Ray said. "They put me in a lineup and that chicken-shit attendant didn't recognize me. He did, I mean, I could tell. But he didn't let on. I just thought you'd like to know. What you said to him must have stuck, ha ha. They asked me what I knew and I said nothing, nothing at all. Hee, hee, hee."

"That's good news, Ray. I appreciate you bringing it by. Can't you get out of the car and come in the house a few minutes? Have a drink?"

"Don't mind if I do," Ray said, and got out of the car. Willis grabbed him and threw him up beside his car and held him by his shirt. Then he hit him in the mouth with his fist about half as hard as he could. Ray went down.

"Jesus, Willis," Ray said. "What's the matter?"

"Keep your goddamn dumb ass away from my house from now on, you dumb piece of shit," Willis said.

Carolyn came outside and saw Willis knock Ray down. She slipped quietly back into the house.

"Someday you'll hit the wrong man, Willis," Ray said, wiping blood from his mouth. "Remember that I told you when it happens." Ray got up and got into his car and drove back down the old dirt road.

Yeah, Willis thought. I've not found the wrong one yet. He laughed and went back toward the house.

* * *

The trees of the forest shuddered and shied away when the monster Broom came near. He was, they sensed, an enemy of life itself, woods and human. He was an agent of death, a destroyer of all peace and happiness.

CHAPTER THREE

How nice it would be to live in a real town, Alice Harper thought as she hung the wash out to dry. How nice it would be to have a washing machine instead of that damned scrub-board. But that would just leave more time to be lonely.

But what a nice morning, she thought. It's almost enough to make you forget your troubles. The date today was May 20, 1950, and it was a beautiful spring day. She could hear the radio through the kitchen window. Ansel and Jody were still asleep and it was at least 9:30. The music was pretty, old-fashioned music from WLOS in Asheville. She had listened to Arthur Godfrey this morning. He had talked about the beautiful weather in New York City.

Alice remembered the time she and Ansel had gone to Atlanta to visit Ansel's sister Oralee and they had all gone out to a nightclub, the Peanut Grove. It had been wonderful. They had danced until late at night, 'til nearly one o'clock. They had wonderful cocktails and dinners. Jody had not come along yet. Those years were too few. It was getting hard to believe there was a world out there beyond the mountains, the world of New York and San Francisco and Paris and Casablanca.

Alice yearned to escape, although she knew that the mountains, the Great Smokies, were beautiful. Tourists came every summer to enjoy the warm days and cool nights of the mountains. They never got as far back in the woods as Waterville Village, of course. They stayed at Lake Junaluska or Maggie Valley. If they only lived closer to Asheville it would be better. As it was they only went to Asheville, where her family lived, every two or three months.

Newport was closer, only fifteen or twenty miles away, down a crooked little blacktop road. The road that went the other way was dirt. It went up past Mt. Sterling School, way up and over Cataloochee to Waynesville. It seemed like the Lord put obstacles in her way. It wasn't that she wasn't grateful for what she had. It was just that she missed her family, she missed having someone to talk to. The neighbors in Waterville Village weren't that friendly. And that was probably for the best. No use getting too thick with them. She did gossip some with Mrs. Cooper, the widow woman who ran the boarding house at the far end of the village. Mrs. Cooper was always good for a juicy tidbit or two.

Like that about Sylvia Mundy. Mrs. Cooper had seen Bob Kelly going to Sylvia's house when her husband, Will, was at work. Bob Kelly was an executive of the power company out of Asheville and didn't live in the village at all, and whenever he came to the plant he seemed to find time to visit Sylvia for an hour or two. Sylvia was a very pretty woman and her husband Will was very ambitious. And sure enough, when the assistant superintendent's job came open, Will moved up into it.

"Sylvia was screwing that Bob Kelly as sure as shit," Mrs. Cooper said, giggling. "Cause you know that Will Mundy is too dumb to be in management."

Alice was shocked at first but she began to understand Sylvia. Sylvia was a nice person. She gave Jody her son's old comic books. Sylvia wanted to move up and out of Waterville Village. And so did Alice.

Alice finished hanging out clothes and it was nearly ten o'clock. She went into the kitchen and started breakfast; bacon and eggs and cream of wheat with milk. She had asked the milkman in her note to leave a small bottle of chocolate milk for Jody. Jody loved it.

She went into the bedroom and shook Ansel awake. Then she went into the smaller bedroom and shook Jody. They both got up and washed their faces and came out to the living room to dress and put on their shoes. The breakfast smelled good and Ansel and Jody were hungry.

"How's your face this morning, Ansel?" Alice asked.

"It's okay," Ansel said.

"Who's Willis Broom, Daddy?" Jody asked.

Ansel and Alice looked at each other.

"He's just a man your daddy knows," Alice said.

"We had some trouble last night, that's all," Ansel said.

"Did he hit your face, Daddy?" Jody asked.

"Yes, he did."

"Did you hit him back?"

"No, son, I didn't."

Jody was puzzled. Gene Autry always beat them up in the movies. Roy Rogers, too. They'd never let anyone get away with that. Jody decided he didn't want to be like his daddy when he grew up. He'd sing pretty like Gene Autry and beat the hell out of them like Roy Rogers.

"Come on to breakfast," Alice said.

After they sat down to eat Alice said, "You say the blessing, Jody."

"God is great. God is good. Let us thank Him for our food. By His hands we all are fed, give us Lord our daily bread. Amen."

"What will you do about Willis, Honey?" Alice asked.

"I don't think I'll need to do anything. I think maybe he got it all out of his system last night."

"I hope you're right," Alice said. But she doubted it.

"I think I'll take Jody-boy here down to Newport for a haircut," Ansel said. "Then maybe this evening we can go to the picture show. What do you think of that, son? Maybe I'll get a haircut, too."

"Oh, goody!" shouted Jody. He would get to see Gene Autry or Roy Rogers. Gene Autry was Jody's favorite.

So they finished their breakfast and walked the long flight of steps and the long sidewalk and across the swinging bridge to the parking lot beside the plant where all the village people kept their cars. Jody hummed and sang all the way. He hated getting a haircut but he loved to go to the movies. He hated haircuts because his daddy always preached to him about holding still while the barber cut his hair. Ansel did that because when Jody got his first haircut, and the barber was almost through, Jody turned his head around to see his daddy and the barber gapped his hair badly. Now he always sat like a little statue. But he hated it anyway.

Ansel and Jody got in the car, and Ansel checked the glove compartment for his gun, a Walther P.38. Jody was scared of that gun, because his daddy had let him pull the trigger once and it went off with a terrible explosion that hurt his ears. It wasn't at all like the guns Gene Autry and Roy Rogers used. Ansel, of course, had been after that very result.

Jody hummed as they went along, the way his mommy hummed and sang in the kitchen.

"Why don't you be quiet for awhile, son? You'll never learn anything if you've always got your mouth working."

Jody tried to sit quietly as the car went down the curves and hills to Newport. But it was hard to do.

In Newport, the barber shop was on the same street as the movie theatre. As Ansel and Jody passed the theatre, Jody pulled his daddy over to the billboards -- Gene Autry in *Springtime in the Rockies*. Jody could read some of it and there were little photographs, stills, of scenes in the movie. Gene on Champion, Gene knocking out the bad men, Gene with the pretty girl. Jody liked the scenes where the horses were running and the men were shooting at each other. That was the most fun. He could hardly wait. They went into the barber shop, where several men were already waiting for a haircut. They sat down on a bench near the front of the shop.

Finally it came Jody's turn to get his hair cut. He hated it, as usual. He had to hold so still he sweated and the sweat ran down in his eyes and the little hairs stuck to his neck. He was miserable.

When the ordeal was over, Ansel paid the two dollars for their haircuts and Jody and Ansel walked out into the warm spring sun. The little hairs on his neck and down his back itched.

"We'll go home and wash up and get the hairs off us, son," Ansel said, "and then we'll come back tonight for the movie."

They got back into the family car, a black '47 Chevrolet Ansel had bought used in January in Newport. As they were driving home, Jody asked his father, "Daddy, why do men have to get haircuts?"

"Because long hair looks bad on a man," Ansel said, "and, too, because everybody gets a haircut now and then. You'd be peculiar-looking if you were the only fellow in town with long hair like a girl's."

Jody sat, trying not to sing. He remembered what his father had said about that. He must know about nearly everything, Jody thought.

At home, Alice had sat down for a few minutes, waiting for Jody and Ansel to return. She was tired. Washing, hanging out the clothes, ironing everything, it all got so tiring and boring. It was the same thing every day, every week. And there was always something that needed to be done. The garden needed planting, the house needed painting, the floors needed mopping. How nice it would be to go out to a movie this evening, even if it was a cowboy movie. She liked movies with Humphrey Bogart, like "Casablanca." That was a really great movie. So romantic.

She got up and turned on the radio. Country music began playing, Hank Snow with "Movin' On." At night she liked to listen to "Suspense" and "Broadway is My Beat." On Saturday Jody always wanted to hear Gene Autry's "Melody Ranch." Alice liked it, too. She liked to hear Gene Autry sing good old songs like "Maria Elana" and "I Don't Want to Set the World on Fire" and such. It all reminded her that there was a world outside Waterville Village, a great, huge world of mystery and adventure.

Not that she didn't love Ansel and Jody. Not at all. She just wanted all the things life had to offer, to experience everything. She shared Ansel's aversion to preachers and such people who wanted to shut out the world and all things foreign and exotic. The Baptist preacher at Woodlawn Baptist Church once even preached against movies and the radio and modern music. She thought that was dumb and ignorant. She had been to the tenth grade and had learned some things. And she could read. She sometimes thought that preachers couldn't read, because if they could they wouldn't be so damned ignorant and backward-looking.

But she did believe in God and Jesus. Jesus to her was a sweet and loving and pleasant man, like her Sunday School teacher, Mr. Munson, when she was a girl. Mr. Munson was so nice and easy-going, and had such loving, forgiving ways. Once she and her childhood friend, Amy Harris, were in the Sunday School room early and had got to saying bad words like "shit" and "damn" and such and Mr. Munson came in and caught them at it. He just laughed and said "shame on you girls" in a laughing, loving way. Alice thought Jesus was that way -- kind, loving, and understanding -- not like most people, church people included. Most people are unforgiving and quick to judge.

She nodded off as she sat listening to the radio, and dreamed. She dreamed that Mr. Munson had come and taken her off to the huge world, to New York and Paris and Casablanca.

There were roads – dirt roads – throughout the Smoky Mountains in the 1950's. They wound side to side and up and down and around and around, following the contours of the mountains. Farmers drove their trucks full of produce very carefully and slowly.

But there were the whiskey-runners who took the booze from the stills, across Cataloochee to Asheville. They drove their souped-up cars at break-neck speed. The trees sensed the danger and the awful fire they threatened to burst into when they ran off the narrow roads. They would slide off the road into the tops of the trees that grew up from the chasm below.

CHAPTER FOUR

Willis's brother Pete Broom pulled the sheriff's car up into the yard of Willis's house on Red Dog. "Red Dog" was the name given to the settlement because the first family to settle on the hard, dry ground in that area had had an old, red hound that was known far and wide as a fabulous hunting dog.

This dog, whose name was Tex, had established his reputation in a bear hunt. He had found the bear – a mountain grizzly, and barked and nipped at him so he treed him – unusual for a grizzly. Tex had kept the bear treed until Willis's grandfather had come and shot it down. The dog was fifteen years old at the time. The old man had named the area "that place where the red dog treed the grizzly," and the Red Dog part stuck. Now several families lived in that area, all farmers.

Carolyn was drying dishes when Pete drove up. She looked out the window and saw him get out of the car and pull his pants up on his belly. She hated Pete almost as much as she did Willis.

"Carolyn?" he called through the screen door. The main door was open. Carolyn pushed her wispy blonde hair out of her eyes with the back of her hand and came into the living room.

"Willis is gone up the hill, Pete," she said flatly. "That's okay," Pete said. "I'll just visit with you a spell."

"Come on in. The screen's unlatched." She knew what would happen. It always did. She was afraid of what Willis would do to her if he found his brother and her together. Maybe, she hoped, they would kill each other.

"You got a beer?" Pete asked, rubbing the roll of fat around his neck with a huge red kerchief. He sat down in the rocker in the living room. Carolyn went to the refrigerator. When she opened the door water poured out the bottom.

"Goddamn it! This damn refrigerator's cut off! Shit!" she said. She pulled out a warm, wet beer and took it to the living room and tossed it to Pete.

"Shit, Carolyn," he protested. "This thing is hot."

She said nothing but went back to the kitchen and got out the mop and mopped the water up and then dried her hands on the wash-rag she had draped over the edge of the kitchen sink.

Pete opened the beer anyway and it spewed out all over him and the floor.

"Warm beer tastes like piss," he mumbled. He could see through the dining room into the kitchen of the small, plain house. Carolyn was bent over wiping up the last of the water and her blue print dress was stuck to her. Pete watched her closely and chugged the beer down as fast as he could to make it seem colder but it didn't help. Carolyn turned around to wipe up the last few spots behind her and Pete could see the curve of her small, white breasts and he felt himself getting excited. It didn't happen to him as often as it used to and when it did he didn't like it to go to waste. He pulled his big ass out of the rocking chair and walked as softly as he could into the kitchen and stood over Carolyn.

She looked up at his bulging crotch and his .38 Smith and Wesson and on up to his fat, sweaty cheeks. He looked to her like a picture she had seen once in a book she had read, *Alice in Wonderland:* he looked like Tweedledum and Tweedledee, the chubby, argumentative twins. She chuckled.

"What's funny?" Pete asked.

"That hat and that uniform you got on; it's right comical, Pete."

"What the hell's comical about it?"

"You ain't no more a sheriff than my ass. You ain't no lawman. You and Willis don't even know right from wrong."

Pete reached down and hauled her up to him and looked her in the eye with a mean look. Then the mean look went soft and he pulled her to him, his left hand on her arm and the right one cupping her butt and pressing her against him. He kissed her, loving her, wanting her desperately.

She could feel him against her and she felt a mixture of emotions. Something about him reminded her of Willis's wild animal fury, which had ruled her life since she met him. The other emotion was revulsion, and it got the upper hand. She pushed him away, though he was much stronger than she, and wiped her mouth where he had kissed her.

Pete backed away and his hat fell off his head and he had to grab for it.

"Someday you'll be sorry, Carolyn," he said, like a hurt little boy.

Carolyn said nothing but just looked at him with as much contempt as she could muster.

"I don't know why Willis would want to marry such a skinny-assed little old thing as you anyway. Listen," he said, composing himself. "I need to talk to Willis. You say he's up on the hill?"

"Moonshining. You going to arrest him?"

"Arrest my baby brother? Naw. I just got to talk to him about some stuff that happened down in Newport. I reckon I'll just go on up there."

"Someday he'll catch you messing with me, Pete."

Pete smiled and walked on through the kitchen and out the back door.

Willis was beside the still, under the old maple tree, dipping a tin cup into the homebrew. He took a long, strong sip and set the cup down on an oak stump. "Willis!" Pete shouted when he saw him.

"Come on up, Pete," Willis said. "Have a snort."

"Might be better than that warm beer I just had down at the house."

"Shit. That damn frigidaire is out again. In the summer that thing tears up about once a week. What you got on your mind, Pete?"

"I just wanted to have a talk with you, little brother. You always have been bad to get in trouble, and I just wanted to let you know, in Newport Sheriff Lane Moss is the law. Not me. I can help you out on this side of the state line, in this county. But when you get in trouble in Tennessee, you're on your own."

"You heard something about me, Pete?"

"I heard you robbed a man at gun point, Willis. That's bad doings. You can get plenty of time in jail for that.

It's big trouble, bigger than I can get you out of. You'd be tried in Newport, in Tennessee."

"Why don't you just worry about what goes on over in this state, Pete? In your county?" Willis looked his brother hard in the eye.

Pete put his foot up on the stump. "What do you reckon Mama would say to you, Willis? You know she wanted both us boys to turn out good."

"So you've turned out good by getting elected sheriff?" Willis said, surly. "Shit. You belong to Jake McConnell and Prentice Hall and that bunch, Pete. Everybody knows it. You've not come up so far in the world. Nobody don't own me. Nobody. Not you, not nobody. So don't bring poor old Mama into this. She had grief from you aplenty while she was alive. Or don't you remember that little episode when you got home out of the service?"

Pete darkened. "Little brother, we've always tried to pull together. That wasn't my fault about Tommy. It was his own doing."

"It broke Mama's heart, Pete. She didn't live a year after that. And who was it told Tommy he could count on him? 'You can count on me', that's what you said, by God. But you weren't there. You see this scar?" He pulled his shirt up to reveal an ugly, white, broad mass of scar tissue that ran from his navel up and around to his side.

"I've seen your scar before, little brother. I couldn't get there. It wasn't my fault. I would have been there if I could."

"Would have, could have, should have. Anyway, Tommy is dead and so is Mama."

Pete took his foot down from the stump and walked away a few steps and then looked back.

"Tommy and you got cut up and I wasn't there. Tommy died. I got to live with that. It don't keep me awake at night. I could arrest you for making whiskey, but I don't. I shut my eyes to a lot. That's how the world is, Willis. I'm just telling you a simple fact. I can help you out of trouble in Haywood County. I can't help you out in Newport. And if you keep carrying that damn gun you're going to get in more trouble than anybody can help you out of. So long, Willis."

Willis took another drink of the fresh moonshine and sat down on the stump. Through the trees he watched Pete walk down the hill and past the house to his deputy's car.

"Damn!" he said, and threw the moonshine to the ground. Tommy had been the second born and Willis had loved him more than he had ever loved anyone in his life. Pete had always been distant since he was ten years older than Willis.

It had been a short-lived mountain feud. Tommy had knocked up Joe Moser's little sister and then dumped her and branded her a slut. Joe got two of his cousins and they came after Tommy to the old home place on Red Dog. Willis had stood with Tommy against them. He took both cousins on himself while Tommy fought Joe. Joe had stabbed Tommy with his huge hunting knife, just once, in the upper abdomen. It had pierced his heart.

He had called out "Pete!" once before he hit the ground and died. Willis had then disabled the two cousins and turned to meet Joe. Joe cut him open and ran off. Willis held his guts in with one hand and drove with the other to the doctor in Newport. One of the cousins died from the head injuries Willis had inflicted on him with just his fists. The other cousin had a broken rib which punctured a lung and rendered him a semi-invalid. The score was figured as even when Joe Moser was sent to prison for ten years, for second-degree murder.

Since then Willis had despised Pete for not showing up to help. Oddly, Pete acquired a reputation as a peaceful man, a sensible person, which was hardly the case. Pete had simply been drunk and slept through the whole fight in a hotel room in Newport with a whore. When he came home to Red Dog Willis told him to get out. He got out, married fat Ida Baker from Balsam, a little town across Cataloochee Mountain, and settled there.

They had four fat kids while Pete did various jobs to make a living. He worked for awhile for Jake McConnell who, along with Prentice Hall, owned most of Haywood County. They decided Pete would be a good man to have in the sheriff's department, so they backed him against an incumbent who was too old for the job anyway.

Rumor was that McConnell and Hall owned Pete because they had something on him which, if it came out, would put Pete in jail for several years. Pete, of course, knew dangerous things about them, too, so their relationship was something like a Mexican standoff.

For example, Pete knew that Hall owned a prostitution house in Balsam, and that McConnell used slave-labor blacks on his dairy farm. But almost everyone knew that, anyway. And McConnell knew that Pete had helped him run a local farmer off his land so he could buy it cheap. He told Pete to scare him off somehow. Pete shot through the living room window with his .30-.30 Remington Rifle, a Christmas present from Ida. The farmer's fourteen-year-old daughter was standing near the window at the time and the bullet went through her chest and out her back into the dining room wall.

Pete was mean; Willis was purely evil. Nobody knew who did it except McConnell and Pete. The girl died and the farmer moved away. From that time on McConnell owned Pete. Pete had come to him and McConnell had taken the rifle. The sheriff at that time, Old John Doughtery – they called him that because he was sixty-eight years old -- dug the bullet out of the dining room wall and promised to find the gun that it came from. He didn't, and McConnell and Hall ran Pete against him the next election, saying Doughtery was incompetent.

As soon as he took office Pete searched the evidence collection, kept in a cardboard box behind the sheriff's desk, found the bullet and threw it away. Still he knew it would never do to cross McConnell. McConnell had money and power enough to buy witnesses against him.

Hall was a different story. A quiet, peaceable man, Hall was a close friend of McConnell – as close a friend as such a man as he could have. Hall owned the prostitutes in Balsam, and he and McConnell owned a printing press which they used to make counterfeit twenties. They sometimes used Pete to pass them in Asheville and Newport, so Pete knew about that. And they knew he passed them, of course, and about the death of the little girl, and about many other things, big and little, that he had done for them.

Pete knew they were more powerful than he, and he knew that when they no longer needed him his tenure as sheriff would be up.

Pete didn't feel corrupt. He was proud to be sheriff and enjoyed the power and authority it gave him. Any smart-ass kid in a fast car might come up against his sap, a little leather bag full of lead buckshot. Once he had even had to shoot a kid that made the mistake of running from him. He shot him twice in the back as he was scrambling up a hill after Pete had slapped him down. The kid had been driving fast around Balsam, blowing his horn. He had had to kill him, the way he figured it.

Willis knew much of this. Most of it, in fact, and he had no real respect for Pete. He knew Pete was proud of being sheriff but he also knew Pete was a possession, a hired hand who did the big boys' dirty work.

Willis sat on the stump until evening shadows began to gather, and then he got up and went down to the can-house and brought back twenty-four Mason jars in a cardboard box and began to fill them from the vat.

The trees of the woods around Mt. Sterling grew restive when they sensed the two Broom brothers talking.

They knew this Willis Broom was dangerous to life.

A gentle rain began and the trees lifted up their branches and leaves. They loved the rain.

CHAPTER FIVE

Willis let the screen door slam behind him. He enjoyed seeing Carolyn jump. It was drawing toward night in Red Dog. And Willis was hungry. Carolyn jumped up from the couch.

"I'll get you some supper in a few minutes, Willis," she said.

"Why the hell ain't you already got supper on the table? You know I don't like waiting around all damned night. Get your ass in the kitchen and fix me some supper or I'll whip your lazy ass."

Carolyn went into the kitchen and opened the broken-down refrigerator, or "ice-box," as they called it, and got some ground beef out of the freezer, which had started to thaw, and went to the pantry for a couple of potatoes. She put the meat in a frying pan and peeled and cut up the potatoes. She poured some of the grease off the meat into another pan and put the potatoes in. She would have to get Woody Rice to come out and fix the ice-box again, she decided. It hadn't been two months since the last time.

The sweat got into her eyes, she was hurrying so fast.

She wiped the sweat away with the back of her hand and put the meat and potatoes into old cracked plates she had got from her mother.

"Supper's ready," she said. "Come and get it."

Willis came into the kitchen and sat down.

"You know," he said, "we got away with that service station money clean. That bastard knew I'd get him if he identified us. We got near five hundred dollars. And I'll make about two hundred and forty dollars from the whiskey that Bryson boy will run for me. I'll have to pay him twenty or thirty dollars. But I'll win it back Saturday night when we play poker at the tavern. Maybe I'll buy some clothes to cover up your cute little ass."

Carolyn was surprisingly good-looking for a woman who had endured so much abuse. She was pleased with even a backhanded compliment from Willis. She ate in silence.

"I busted Harper's face last night. One of these days I'm going to kill him. But first I'll let him sweat and worry about it. I'm going to beat him half to death and then finish him off with my little buddy, here." He slapped the .38 S&W under his belt.

He will have to be stopped someday, Carolyn thought. Just stopped. He hadn't been so bad when she first met him. He had been young and strong and tall and good-looking in a rough way. Now he was fat and sloppy, like a boar hog, she thought. She should have seen it then, his craziness, his wildness and his meanness. She had found him exciting at first. His cruelty she had smoothed over in her own mind because he was protective of her. He had a fast car and a few dollars in his pocket when they met, and she had been so poor and her father had abused her so that she had come to expect such treatment as normal. But she had, over the years, come to realize the abnormality of her life and existence. Especially since she had met such nice people as Ansel and Alice Harper. She knew Ansel would never beat Alice.

Willis got up from the table and walked outside and into the woods toward his still.

Carolyn carried the dishes into the kitchen and began to wash them. She wished she had married someone like Ansel Harper, a nice, steady guy who wouldn't slap her around. Someone to have children for. Willis had beaten her during her first pregnancy and she lost the baby and couldn't have any more. She hated Willis but Willis was all she had. Her family was too sorry to go back to.

And now he says all the time how he's going to kill Ansel Harper, she thought. He was really drunk on the job and he knew it. He should have been fired. But he blamed Ansel for telling on him and he held a grudge forever. She thought about warning Ansel, but she was afraid Willis would kill her if she did.

She heard a car driving up the dirt road that led from the paved road to Newport to the house. She went out. It was Johnny Bryson in his '49 Ford.

Johnny raced his motor for Carolyn's benefit and then shut if off and got out and came up on the porch.

"Willis around?" he asked.

"He's up in the woods right now. You can go up and find him or you can wait here 'til he comes back. Whichever," she said.

Johnny thought Carolyn was a beautiful woman. She was older, in her thirties, and he was in his early twenties. He wanted to get hold of her and kiss her. He ached with desire for her. But he knew Willis would kill him if he did anything. He knew Willis was mean.

Johnny decided to wait for Willis. He came in the house, following behind Carolyn through the screen door. He reached out and touched her arm and she turned around and looked up, at him and he decided to be brave. He put his hands on her arms and drew her slowly closer and closer until she was right up in his face. She didn't holler or turn away and so he kissed her very softly on her mouth. She closed her eyes and let him.

And then she pulled away. "You'd better not do that no more," she said.

"I better go look for Willis, I guess.

"Maybe you better," Carolyn said.

Johnny went on outside and up the path behind the house to the still.

What a nice kiss, Carolyn thought as he left. But he's got a wife and three little kids, and he's risking his life for a kiss. It made her feel proud and warm inside. It was a good feeling to be wanted, and she knew Johnny wanted her. But he's too nice a boy to get killed over me, she decided, and went back to cleaning the house.

Johnny went up over the hill through the woods and came upon Willis putting fruit jars of moonshine into two cardboard boxes.

"Hey-o, Willis," Johnny said.

Willis jumped. "Goddamn it, boy, don't come upon me like that. I could have shot the shit out of you."

"Have you got me a load to haul, Willis?"

"Sure do," he said, putting the last jar in the box. "Two cases. Two hundred and forty dollars' worth. You haul it for me and I'll pay you twenty or so when you get back with the money."

"Sure thing," Johnny said. "Here, I'll carry one box if you'll get that one."

They carried the whiskey down to Johnny's car. The Ford's rear end sat up high off the ground on good springs so that the car would look normal when it was loaded with whiskey. They loaded the whiskey into the trunk and closed the lid.

"Here's the address in Asheville where you got to go to unload it. Don't get caught. Whatever the law does to you, I'll do worse. You understand?

"I'll be back Saturday," Johnny said.

"Why not tomorrow?" Willis asked.

"I want to have a little fun in Asheville. I don't want to just hurry-ass there and hurry-ass back."

"Saturday, then. Don't spend any of that money before you get back or I'll stomp a mudhole in your ass."

"See you Saturday, Willis."

Willis turned back to the house and Johnny hopped into his Ford and roared off down the road.

Willis came in the house where Carolyn was sweeping. "Poor dumb bastard," he said. "He takes all the risk and I make all the money."

Carolyn continued sweeping, saying nothing.

"Hey, listen to me when I talk to you."

"I'm sorry," she said. "I heard what you said."

"Well, act like it. I put the food on the table, don't I? Who's the damn boss in this house, anyway?"

"You, Willis," she said. Someday someone will fix your fat, mean ass, she thought.

The trees were concerned by the awful danger of the Broom brothers and for the woman, Carolyn. But the rain comforted them. They luxuriated in the sweet downpour and sang together happily, softly, a song no human being could hear.

CHAPTER SIX

Johnny's Ford slid around the curve in the dirt road that led across Cataloochee toward Waterville Village. He laughed to think how easily he had got away from the Asheville police.

"Sweetheart," he said, kissing his steering wheel and patting it, "you're the sweetest lil' ol' car on the roads. That you are."

He felt in his shirt pocket the wad of bills, dampened by sweat, that Faircloth had given him in exchange for the moonshine. It was a shame most of it would go to Willis. He began to sing "Lovesick Blues."

He passed a bumpy side road and swore under his breath as he saw Pete Broom's police car, a '50 Chevy, painted black and white by Pete himself. Pete had had to supply his own car. Jake McConnell had helped out. McConnell wanted his hired help to look official.

The siren had cost Pete fifty dollars of his own money, but it was loud. Johnny swore again and slowed his whiskey car down to twenty, to ten and pulled over. Pete pulled up behind him on the grassy bank on the side of the road.

Pete walked up to Johnny's side of the car. "Driving a little wild, ain't you, sonny?"

"Sorry, sheriff. I wanted to get home before dark. Sarah don't like to stay at home by herself."

"Let's see your license, boy," Pete said.

"You know I ain't got one, Pete. About nobody does back in here. You probably ain't even got one yourself."

"Get out," Pete said. He punched Johnny in the stomach and doubled him over and then brought his knee up into Johnny's face.

"Smart-alecky talk don't go unnoticed by the sheriff's office, boy. You better go back to 'yes, sir' and 'no, sir'. What you got in your pocket, there, Johnny?"

"That goes to Willis."

Pete put his hand up to get the money and Johnny stepped back. Pete looked at him and something in his eyes convinced Johnny to stand still. Pete took the money out and counted it.

"Two hundred and forty dollars. How much is yours and how much goes to Willis?"

"Willis gets the two hundred. I get the forty."

"You mean you were feeling that good, riding along like a goddamn fool, all for forty dollars?"

"Yes, sir," Johnny said.

"Well, I'm fining you twenty dollars for driving at an unsafe rate of speed and driving without a license. That ought to cool you down some."

Pete stuck the rest of the money back in Johnny's shirt and left him leaning against his car looking down.

"Bastard," Johnny muttered under his breath. Pete didn't hear him and walked back to his car and drove away, sliding in the dirt.

Johnny got back into his car and pulled off slowly. He knew Pete could get away with it. It was just the way things were. Why worry about it? Johnny thought as he drove on over the dirt road toward Waterville Village and Newport.

Sarah had the radio on as she swept out the living room. The linoleum was cracked and bent and curled up and dirt was caught in it. It was a hopeless task to try to clean the house, especially with three kids around. And Johnny was just a big kid, driving moonshine all over the Smokies.

Sarah wondered as she swept how she managed to get herself in such a predicament. She had come from a pretty nice family in Newport. Now her mother was dead and her father had just gone senile. He just wandered around the house, mumbling to himself about the past. The house had grown up in vines and bushes and he never shaved or took a bath any more. He never even worked in the garden. He was just weak-minded since Sarah's mother had died and he was no good for anything. He couldn't help Sarah any. The small amount of retirement money he got went for beer and food. Sarah could always count on her mother to help when she was alive. Sarah's father couldn't help her. He was barely there for himself.

It had broken Sarah's heart to watch it happen to them. It seemed to her that life was an awful cheat. She wondered if it seemed that way to other people.

She leaned her broom against the refrigerator, which hummed and grumbled all the time, and washed her hands in the kitchen sink and when she tried to turn the water off the faucet continued a steady drip.

"Oh!" she said, and pushed it hard. She felt it give and the faucet bent backwards and water spurted out into her face and into the air.

Sarah put her hands up to her face and cried aloud. Then she grabbed the rag that hung on the old iron kitchen stove and tried to stop the water. Finally she looked under the sink and cut the water off there. She stood back and surveyed the damage and began to weep silently.

"Mommy! Mommy!" Johnny Junior cried, running into the kitchen from the back yard, with Laura Mae and Cindy behind him. "What happened, Mommy?"

"The sink tore up. You three run out to the wood pile and get me a big stick of wood apiece, okay? Mommy's got to start dinner. Your daddy will be home in an hour or so."

She never knew exactly when Johnny would show up, but it was usually about six o'clock, give or take thirty minutes.

The children ran out and down the hill to the woodpile that Johnny had piled up last autumn before the weather got cold. The wood was mostly jack pine and balsam with some hickory for kindling. Sarah watched them as they came puffing back up the hill, each carrying a piece of wood as heavy as he or she could carry.

She felt a tickle deep in her throat, down in her lungs, and she began to cough. Tears came to her eyes and she coughed and coughed, a dry, rasping cough until she had to go to the living room and sit down. She didn't like thinking about it but it sounded like the same cough her mother had had before the doctor told her she had cancer.

Sarah was afraid to go to the doctor because of what he might say. The coughing spells only came every other day or so and then she coughed so hard she saw stars and got dizzy and had to sit down. She had lost ten pounds last month when she had weighed herself on the Toledo scales in Nelson's Drug Store in Newport. She didn't know how much she had lost since then. And there was no big mirror in the house except the bathroom mirror. In that she could only see her face and she seemed to have bags under her eyes.

Maybe it's just my nerves, she thought hopefully. She got out the corn meal and mixed some water in it and beat the mixture up with a tablespoon. Then she got the lard can out and took the spoon and dipped out two big spoonfuls of lard and whacked the spoon onto the black skillet on the stove until the lard came off the spoon.

The children came in with the wood and she put each stick into the stove and got a big Diamond kitchen match and lit a piece of newspaper and dropped it into the stove and closed the door.

She opened the refrigerator door and bent down and got out a head of lettuce and tore off several leaves of it and dropped them into a ceramic bowl. The fire melted the lard and it began to smoke so she closed the damper and picked up the frying pan and poured the hot grease directly onto the lettuce. Johnny loved "killed" lettuce, as they called it. And corn bread fritters.

Then she realized that he might not be home for half an hour so she set the grease back down on the stove and mixed the corn meal up and cracked an egg into it. An egg always made corn bread taste better. Then she poured the mixture into the frying pan. It crackled and popped and smelled good. Or it would have smelled good to Sarah, but her appetite had been off the last few days.

If Johnny was too late she would kill the lettuce again. Johnny always liked to come in and get a beer and sit in his favorite chair and listen to the radio for a few minutes before they ate. Sarah always tried to plan it so Johnny could do that. She liked to please him. Johnny was really all she had, now. Her older sister had moved away to Dayton, Ohio, where her husband had gone to work in a rubber plant. When she had lived in Newport, her sister, Mildred, would take the kids now and then to give her a breathing spell. And her Mom would have done the same thing.

Now there was nobody.

What the hell am I going to do when I need some water out of the damn kitchen faucet? she wondered. Maybe Johnny will fix it when he gets in. After dinner.

She opened the refrigerator again and took out the pork chops. She put some more lard in a small frying pan and laid the pork chops into it. Then she heard the rumble of Johnny's Ford coming up the dirt road into the yard. "Varroom, varroom!" the car went.

The next day, Saturday, Johnny drove to Red Dog to give Willis his money. He told Willis what Pete had done.

"Long as he don't steal from me," Willis said, giving Johnny the remaining twenty dollars.

"He's your brother, Willis," Johnny protested. "That don't mean I have to make good his fee-grabbing. Sorry, Johnny."

"Well, at least he didn't get it all," Johnny said. His mouth was dry with anger. But he saw the handle of the .38 protruding from Willis's belt.

"You comin' to play cards tonight, Johnny?" Willis asked as Johnny folded the money and put it in his pocket.

"Sure thing," Johnny said. "Wouldn't miss it. Give me a chance to get some more of that whiskey money."

Johnny laughed lamely and Willis did, too.

Stupid young bastard, Willis thought.

So that night they all gathered in the back room of Beck's Tavern, Willis with his two hundred dollars, Johnny with his twenty dollars, and Frank and

Rufus with five hundred apiece to gamble with. They played seven card draw poker.

By about ten o'clock Johnny was doing very well. He had won a big pot with a straight flush and now the pot was growing again. The draw went his way again and now Johnny had won all of Willis's money and most of Frank's and Rufus's.

"I'm quitting, fellers," Johnny said. "I've got to go on home. Babies need a new pair of shoes ha, ha."

"You'd better set your ass back down and give me a chance to win my money back," Willis said.

"Sorry, Willis. I always try to quit while I'm ahead."

"You could have a chance at the rest of our money," Rufus said. "Willis is busted anyway, ain't you, Willis?"

"I got ten more dollars in my pocket," Willis said.

"Thanks anyway, boys," Johnny said. "I got to go home."

"I guess I'll quit, too," Willis said.

Willis followed Johnny through the tavern where several men and a couple of girls were drinking and dancing.

"Hey, Johnny!" Willis shouted above the din of the tavern. "Let's go down to Juny's and get us a few drinks, what do you say?"

"No thanks, Willis," Johnny said, and kept walking toward the front door. "I got to go home."

"Well, hell, come on home with me and have a few drinks. You ought to celebrate. You must have won close to five hundred dollars. Most of it off me. You should celebrate a little."

"I'd like to," Johnny said, going on out the door and toward the parking lot, "but I got to get on home."

"Go on, then, and be goddamned!" Willis shouted. Johnny got in his Ford and screeched away.

Willis was fuming. I'll get that stupid young bastard for that, he said to himself.

An old Plymouth drove into the parking lot. It was Jeff and Ray. They saw Willis standing beside his truck and drove over beside him.

"What you doing tonight, Willis? Let's go have some fun."

"Sure as hell, I'm plenty ready," Willis said, and jumped into the back seat of the Plymouth, leaving his Chevy truck in the tavern parking lot. They screeched away like Johnny had. Like mischievous teenagers.

"Let's go to the Hot Spot and have a few drinks," Jeff said. "Then who knows where we might go from there?"

They drove to the other side of Newport and pulled up in the Hot Spot's parking area and went in. The place was wild and loud, beer was a quarter and whiskey was fifty cents a glass, not too bad for 1950. They sat at a booth and looked around until they spotted a loud-mouthed little fat man who was flirting with a waitress. He looked and acted like someone with money to throw around. They saw him shove a five-dollar bill down the low-cut blouse of the waitress, and they looked at each other and grinned.

Ray got up and went over to the little man's table.

"Hey, buddy," Ray said, "why don't you come over and join us. We got a proposition for you."

"Hell," the little man said, "why not?"

They could tell he wasn't a native.

"Where you from, little buddy?" Jeff asked.

"I'm from Saddle River, New Jersey," he said. "I'm a salesman with the Concord Electrical Motor Corporation. I travel all over the country."

"How about that," Willis said. "You're just the fellow we wanted to talk to. Yeah. Tell me, Mr. --?"

"Milbrook. Henry Milbrook, at your service, gentlemen."

"Ha, ha, Mr. Milbrook. Tell us, do you ever like to gamble? Play a little poker?"

"Oh, yes. You have a game around here?"

"Sure as hell do," Willis said. "You want to join us? We'll show you some real Southern hospitality."

"Well, why not?" said Milbrook. "Let's go."

They all piled into Milbrook's Ford station wagon. "We'll show you where to go, Mr. Milbrook," Ray said. "Here, have some real mountain moonshine."

Milbrook took a big drink of the whiskey and lost his breath. "God-All-Mighty!" he wheezed, and they all had a good laugh.

They directed Milbrook off the main highway onto a little dirt road into the deep woods. It was like a washboard. Milbrook began to worry.

"Hey, fellas. Where the hell are we going, anyway?"

"Just a mile or two more," Ray said. "You'll like it when you see it."

Sure enough, they came out beside the river. The moon was beautiful on the water. It was cool, about twelve o'clock. The mountains are always cool at night, even in July and August.

They piled out of the station wagon and Ray and Jeff gathered up some wood for a fire. Willis talked to Milbrook.

"What kind of shit do you do for this goddamn electrical motor company, Milbrook?"

"I represent the company and sell motors to companies that need them. Big ones, little ones, all kinds in between." He was getting a little bit nervous and was sobering up a little.

"Have another pull on this jug, Milbrook. You sound like you're about to sober up."

"I don't really hold my liquor too well," Milbrook said.

"Hey, here's the cards. You cut for the deal, Willis," Ray said.

Willis dealt first. The fire was going good. It was a big fire.

Milbrook started off losing but then he caught up. Willis was out of the game so he lay down on the opposite side of the campfire from the card players.

Pretty soon Milbrook won quite a bit. He took out his wallet to put the money in and Ray and Jeff saw the thick sheaf of bills that looked like twenties and fifties.

After another hand, when Milbrook won, Willis said, "Hey! I believe Mr. Milbrook is cheating, don't you, fellers?"

"Yeah," Ray said. "And I was just thinking what a good ol' boy he was, too."

"Yeah," Jeff said. "You're sure a goddamn disappointment, Mr. Milbrook."

"I think we ought to teach him better than that," Willis said, drawing his .38.

Milbrook panicked and stood up. "I'm leaving," he said.

"No, you ain't," said Willis, and shot him in the head. He fell face down into the fire.

Ray and Jeff emptied his pockets of money except for a few dollars and change. They left him with his head in the fire, burning.

Willis and Ray and Jeff divided up the little fat man's money, about five hundred dollars in cash. They left Willis at his truck at the tavern and took the station wagon back to the Hot Spot. Jeff drove Milbrook's station wagon back up to the campsite and Ray drove their Plymouth behind him. They left Milbrook's station wagon at the campsite and then both left in their Plymouth.

Willis came home to Carolyn about two o'clock in the morning and woke her up to have sex. He felt exhilarated and he had nearly two hundred dollars in his pocket. You can't beat old Willis Broom, he thought, as he drifted off to sleep beside his wife.

When morning came it began to rain. Milbrook still lay face down in the campfire with most of his face and head burned away. The small bullet hole was no longer visible. The morning rain washed the ashes down the bank and into the river.

There were many souls in the trees in the green forest that were once Cherokee, now long dead. Some remembered the awful time when they were marched away from these glorious, beautiful mountains to an ugly place far away where there was no shade from the sun and so many died. Some had died on the way, some had lived out their years in the new land. Many of their souls found their way back to the Smoky Mountains.

They watched the fat man with the gun, whom they feared almost as much as fire itself.

One tall old pine tree which held within it the soul of a Cherokee warrior spoke:

> "O my children! My poor children!
> Listen to the words of wisdom,
> Listen to the words of warning,
> From the lips of the Great Spirit, from the Master of Life, who made you.
> I have given you lands to hunt in,
> I have given you bear and bison, …
> Filled the rivers full of fishes;
> Why then will you hunt each other?"

CHAPTER SEVEN

Johnny revved the powerful motor of his '49 Ford. There were two cases of whiskey in the car's small trunk. Johnny knew it would take the turns in the curvy mountain road with ease. The car seemed built for just such a job as this, with its powerful engine and sleek shape. He could outrun anyone in competition with him for the Asheville business.

He started off up the dirt road across Cataloochee to Asheville. The car raised a trail of dust from the road. It was Monday morning and he was feeling good. He had won nearly five hundred dollars Saturday night and he would earn forty more today. Pretty soon he'd have enough for Sarah some new furniture and a washing machine and a paint job for his Ford. He loved his car. It was moss green now but he wanted it painted black. And there were dents in it from some of the close calls he had had.

Once an Asheville policeman had got after him just as he was getting into town. He screeched off around a corner and hit a parked car on the other side of the street.

He remembered with glee the time Sheriff Lane Moss, the Cocke County sheriff, had got after him going west out of Newport. Johnny had spun rocks and raised hell and slid around in the road, scratching up the car, but he had got clean away.

As Johnny navigated the winding road he thought of Carolyn Broom, for no reason. She just popped into his mind. That woman does something to me, he said to himself. Why do the most beautiful girls wind up with the meanest sons-of-bitches? What a shame Willis has got her, he thought, and drove on over the mountain.

Monday morning brought Carolyn and Willis out of bed early, although on this day Willis didn't have to go to work. He went out to the still, thinking about the money he'd lost to Johnny. It infuriated him. He began to think, slowly and stupidly, and to plot.

After awhile he came back down from the still to the house. He had something on his mind.

Johnny drove down the far side of Cataloochee Mountain into Asheville. He slowed down to the city speed limit of thirty-five. In Tennessee there was no speed limit. The signs just said, "Drive with Care." He didn't want to attract any attention.

But, as luck would have it, as he was driving into Asheville, a black-and-white police car came out from behind an old brick building and settled in behind him, stalking him. He gunned his motor. His tires screeched on the blacktop pavement and he sped away.

The police car sped after him. It was also a '49 Ford, souped up for just such an occasion.

Johnny looked back through his rear-view mirror at the police car gaining on him. Damn! he thought to himself. I don't need to get caught with this big a load. He looked for an alleyway to turn into. Before long he found one and turned, his tires screeching on the street. It was a one-way street going the other way. He met a car coming in the other side and barely made it past him. The police car following him didn't make it. It slammed into the other car and Johnny went on his way, driving slower now.

His engine was so powerful it made a heavy roaring noise even when he went slowly. He needed a new muffler. The one he had added to the noise and attracted attention.

He pulled into Grant's warehouse at ten a.m. and got out and went to the office.

"That delivery from Newport is here. You might want to tell Mr. Grant," he said to the old guy on duty.

In a few minutes the old guy brought Mr. Grant. Grant went to Johnny's car and Johnny opened the trunk for him. They unloaded the whiskey and Grant opened his wallet and took out two one-hundred dollar bills and two twenties and gave them to Johnny.

"Thanks a lot," Johnny said. Forty for me and two hundred for Luke Malone in Newport. He liked dealing with Luke. Luke always paid him fair and square, not hum-hawing around like Willis.

He knew Willis wanted to win that poker money off him. Johnny chuckled with delight. When this trip was over he'd have a little more than five hundred dollars saved up. He'd maybe take Sarah and the kids to the Sears Roebuck store in Asheville or maybe they'd order from the big Spring catalog. Hot stuff, Johnny thought. Then Sarah wouldn't mind his fooling around so much. She probably knew more than she let on.

Johnny got back in his car, the rear end sitting high up off the ground now, and drove conservatively out of Asheville toward Cataloochee.

Cataloochee was one of the wrinkles in the aging face of earth. The trees were green and the woods stretched as far as the eye could see. Johnny thought what beautiful scenery this was. He reckoned it was the most beautiful country on earth. He had not seen much of the world. He had been too young for service in the Second World War so he didn't get to see Europe or the South Pacific. Still he thought these green mountain shadows were the prettiest thing there was. He had seen the flat land, down in Raleigh and in South Carolina when he had delivered moonshine to those places.

The noonday sun was hot on him and he had his windows rolled down. Up the road he saw another car coming his way from the cloud of dust it stirred up,

Both cars slowed down because the road was so narrow. Johnny recognized Ray Moore as they drew closer. Ray was in his old Plymouth and was drunk as usual.

"Hey, boy," Ray said. "Coming back from Asheville? Carry a load of 'shine over there?"

"No comment, Ray," Johnny laughed.

They were shouting from their cars.

"Come on and hop out and have a drink. You haul that stuff so you should drink some of it yourself."

Johnny pulled his car over and got out. Ray got out of his car with a bottle and they passed the bottle back and forth.

"Good stuff," said Johnny.

"Pure corn whiskey," Ray said. "Good for what ails you."

"You headed to Asheville, Ray?" Johnny asked.

"Sure am. I'm just going for a good time. I ain't hauling anything. I came into some money Saturday night."

"Did you hear about that New Jersey feller they found up above Red Dog? Had a heart attack and fell in his own fire. His face and head was mostly burned away."

"Yeah, I heard about it," Ray said. "The sheriff said it must have been a heart attack. He was a fat little feller, anyway. Jeff and Willis and I met him that night. He was overweight. That's what killed him, all right."

"How'd you come into some money? Maybe I'll look in the same place," Johnny said.

"Oh, you know. Do somebody a favor and it comes back to you. Cast your bread on the water. You know?"

"Ain't talking, huh?" Johnny said. "Well, okay. I got to get on down the road. Have a good time in Asheville."

"Will do. So long," Ray said.

Johnny thought to himself as he drove away that he bet he knew where Ray had got the money. That little fat feller from New Jersey. What a mean-assed bunch that Jeff and Ray and Willis made, Johnny thought. He'd hate to cross them.

Then he realized he'd already crossed Willis, when he won all that money off him. But Willis hadn't pulled anything so far. He figured he didn't have anything to worry about. He drove on home to Newport.

Johnny got home to Sarah and the kids by about two o'clock p.m. Sarah had not started supper yet. She came to the door as he drove up and kissed him as he came in.

"Have you gone by Luke's place yet, Johnny?" Sarah asked.

"Not yet. You want to go over there with me? We'll eat downtown at Tingle's. What do you say to that?"

"What'll we do with the kids? Take them with us?"

"Naw. I tell you what. We'll give old Mrs. Caldwell a couple of dollars to keep them. Okay?"

"Oh, Johnny, that'd be so nice, to eat out for a change. I'll get the kids ready."

She got the kids into the house and cleaned them up. Mrs. Caldwell had a chicken farm so they'd probably all come back with chicken shit all over them. But God! It'd be worth it to get out of the house for a change.

They all piled into Johnny's Ford and drove down the road to Mrs. Caldwell's to drop off the kids and then drove on toward town. Sarah had never left the kids with any one besides her mother and her sister and she felt a little guilty.

"Do you reckon she'll feed them, Johnny?" she asked.

"Sure. She's a fine old lady. We'll have to do this more often."

Sarah fairly glowed inside.

They stopped by Luke Malone's house just inside the Newport city limits. Johnny gave Luke the two hundred and forty dollars and Luke paid him forty. Johnny gave it to Sarah and she giggled and kissed the picture of Andrew Jackson.

Then they drove on down into Newport. They went to Rogers' Hardware store and looked around awhile. Then they went to Smith's Furniture and bought a new chest of drawers, and from there they went to the Belk store and bought two cute little outfits for the girls and some cowboy boots for Johnny, Jr. They even bought a new dress for Sarah.

"Let's go have a hot dog at Nelson's Drugstore, Honey," Sarah said. She loved drug store hot dogs. They even got a milkshake. It was so good they got another and shared it. Sarah was so happy. And Johnny had plenty of money left.

"Let's put it in the bank, Johnny," Sarah said.

"No," Johnny said. "I don't like to have my money tied up in the bank. I'm thinking of getting another car. A new '50 Ford I saw at Seals' Ford place."

"You just bought the car we got, Johnny. Please let's put it in the bank."

"Maybe next week. I got some things I want to buy."

Sarah sat quietly as Johnny sucked the last of the milkshake up through the straw with a braak sound. She knew it was too much to ask Johnny to save some money. He had never saved anything and never would. Oh, well, she thought. He was generous when he had it to give.

Johnny looked at Sarah. She was pale and thin and sickly-looking, with bags under her eyes. He thought how much better looking Carolyn Broom was. But he had married Sarah for better or for worse and he tried to be good to her, except for some fooling around. And what man didn't?

They looked around in the drug store and then went to the Rose's 5 and 10 cent store on Railroad Street. After they looked around there and bought some toys for the kids it was time for supper. They went to Tingle's and ordered a club sandwich for Sarah and a chopped Sirloin for Johnny. They had a good time.

But still Johnny was thinking about Carolyn Broom.

They finished eating and walked down to see what was on at the Ritz. It was an all-cartoon movie, "Snow White and the Seven Dwarfs."

"It's too bad we don't have the kids with us," Sarah said. They walked back to the car and went home, picking up the kids on the way. It was getting towards dark so they told the kids they'd have to come inside the house pretty soon.

With the kids outside, Johnny approached Sarah for a little loving. "How about a little lovin'?" he asked Sarah.

"Okay," she said.

They lay drowsing off into sleep when the phone rang.

Johnny answered it. It was Lon Tingen, a farmer who made moonshine. Tingen wanted him to haul a big load to Asheville. A big load was forty-eight quart-jars full, two cases, and it brought nearly five hundred dollars. It was all his trunk would hold.

Johnny came back in the bedroom.

"I've got to go pick up a big load from Lon Tingen and take it over to Asheville."

"I wish you could make more money fixing cars. You're real good at it, Johnny. You don't have to risk your life and your freedom to run that liquor."

"This is easy money, Sugar. I can't turn it down."

Johnny dressed and hopped into his car. He had a mental picture of his wife lying naked from the waist down on their big feather bed. Still he couldn't help wondering what Carolyn Broom would look like that way.

The trees whispered to one another when Johnny was driving up Cataloochee. They sensed that Johnny would die violently.

CHAPTER EIGHT

Sarah watched Johnny speed away. He sure likes to drive wild, Sarah thought. That wildness was probably what she loved about him. Though they were poor, they were happy. He didn't really have to run liquor over the mountain roads to Asheville. But he enjoyed the thrill of it.

She left the window and went back to the bedroom to get her panties and skirt. She pulled them on lethargically and went out on the porch to call the kids in.

Johnny will probably be gone all night and would get in early next morning. It didn't matter much what day it was. She felt badly. She felt sick. She had found blood in her urine, and she knew she should see a doctor, but money was not coming in very steadily. Johnny would bring in good money one week and nothing the next. And he'd always spend it on his car, for new tires or a new transmission or something.

What am I supposed to do? she asked herself. What? She had three kids to clothe and feed. How was she supposed to do that on what Johnny brought in? And now I've got some kind of sickness. We don't have any insurance, she thought. I can't afford to get sick.

"Junior! Laura Mae! Cindy! Come on in the house! It's getting dark!"

They ran into the house and little Cindy's pants were wet so Sarah changed her clothes. The other two were nasty as pigs but she left them alone. No company coming, she thought.

There was never any company. That was one thing that was wrong. They never had company. Not like things were when she lived at home with her folks, before her mother died. Company was over all the time. Usually it was somebody they knew from church.

Now they never went to church and there was never company. There seemed to be no reason to get cleaned up. What's the use when you never see anybody? And Johnny was gone at all hours and often slept through the day.

She remembered the time Johnny first came to see her. She had met him in town with her girlfriend, Cathy Mears. Cathy was struck on Johnny's friend Cecil Upchurch and Cecil never went anywhere without Johnny. They met at Frye's Soda Shop one fall day seven years ago. Cecil and Johnny and Cathy and Sarah. The weather was a magic autumn, cool, brisk but very pleasant, and Sarah had on a tight sweater. She knew Johnny noticed her breasts because he couldn't take his eyes off them. He didn't look at her like that much anymore. Maybe he didn't love her any more. She had lost weight lately and there were bags under her eyes. Not like when she was fifteen.

Johnny had asked her to go to a movie. It was "Boom Town" with Clark Gable. She wanted to go but her father wouldn't tolerate movies. They were of the devil, he said. He'd never been to one, Sarah had thought then, so he didn't have any way of knowing whether they were sinful or not. He also thought soda pop was of the devil. The preacher had preached on that very topic.

Sarah never really liked going to church. The preacher was so boring. She liked Sunday School because of the Bible stories, but she used to go to sleep during the sermon, at least until the preacher would bellow out "Amen!" or something. She missed church, though, because you made good friends you could trust at church. Except maybe for Cathy Mears. Cathy had tried to steal Johnny away from her.

That had happened after they had been going together for about six months. Cecil Upchurch had joined the army. Everyone was surprised that he was smart enough to get in. And Cathy turned her eyes toward Johnny. She flirted with him and Johnny gave in and took her out.

Johnny always liked fast cars and when he came to pick Sarah up for a date he would gun his motor while he waited for her. He never came into the house until just before they had got married.

Sarah felt a pain low in her stomach and became nauseous. She went to the bathroom and threw up. It seemed like nothing she ate would stay down.

Johnny had been so good-looking back then. He was getting a beer belly now, but he still was handsome and wild. She loved to ride with him in the Ford with the windows down and the wind flapping his hair around. It was beautiful, coarse dark hair.

She sat down in the living room and turned on the radio. It was dark outside now but the kids still wanted to stay up and play. She settled back on the couch drowsily. As she went to sleep she thought of her Johnny, somewhere out on the lonesome mountain road that went up Cataloochee. The radio was tuned to WLOS, Asheville, North Carolina, and it played "I'm so Lonesome I Could Cry" by Hank Williams. That's how lonesome I am, she thought as she sank into sleep.

Johnny was indeed on the road that went up Cataloochee. He was driving along with the car radio on. He was listening to Hank Williams, too. He added up his money in his head and got close to a thousand dollars. He knew he would spend it on his family. But he thought about how far that money would get him with Carolyn Broom.

He couldn't get Carolyn off his mind. When he thought of her a certain way he ached, literally ached.

Willis is getting older, Johnny thought. He must be up around forty. And he's mean. He's probably mean to Carolyn. He had often seen her with bruises on her face and arms. Once he saw her with white shorts on, and she had a big bruise on her left thigh, on the outside, like she'd been kicked.

I could take her away from him, Johnny thought, if only I weren't saddled with Sarah and three kids. I got four people depending on me. And Sarah looks sickly lately.

He went on over Cataloochee and into Asheville. He took the load to Grant and got the five hundred. He would get sixty out of it. He had already added that in, in his head. But maybe he could spend a little in town. It was getting late, around ten o'clock, when he left Grant's warehouse. He looked around town for some action.

He passed a little road house on the outside of Asheville called the Beehive. It looked sleazy, and that was what he was in the mood for. Carolyn was a little bit sleazy. Just a little bit. And there was danger there, too, in the form of Willis Broom.

He decided as he pulled into the Beehive that he would go after Carolyn all the way, all the damn way, when he got back to Newport.

He cut off the motor and got out of the car. He didn't lock the door in case he had to get away in a hurry. The front door of the place was shiny red and the little brick building was shiny blue. Tacky as hell, Johnny thought.

Just what the doctor ordered.

He opened the door and went in. The place was loud, dark and smoky. The odor of stale beer and piss permeated the place. It was crowded with men and women and boys and girls, all rubbing up against each other. He squeezed his way to the bar and got a beer.

Two girls came over to him. They were obviously girlfriends cautiously sizing him up. They looked married, somehow, Johnny thought. One was chomping on bubble gum.

"Whaddya say, Big Boy?" the blonde said.

"Nothing much," Johnny replied. "How's business?"

"Screw you, Jack," the blonde replied, and both of them moved away.

Some drunk had the music up high and was trying to dance to a country song -- "Moving On" by Hank Snow. He was clumsy, bumping into everybody. He backed into Johnny and kicked him on the shin. Johnny had been waiting for him to do that. He spun the drunk around and hit him in the face and the drunk went down and out.

"Hey, kid, why'd you do that?" a fat man asked, and took a swing at Johnny. He missed and fell into a table with two men and two women and one of the men hit the fat man. Pretty soon half the people in the Beehive were fighting. Johnny left without a scratch. As he was leaving a pretty doe-eyed girl, with black hair like his own, stared up at him.

"You leaving before the fun's over?" she asked.

"Best time to go. Come with me?" Johnny asked.

"Sure. Where to?"

"We'll get a room at the Carolina Hotel," he said.

"You get right to the point," she said, "down to the nitty-gritty, don't you?"

"No use wasting time. Time's precious."

"We'll see whether we're wasting time when we get there," she said.

He got a room, a single, and she came up a few minutes later.

"I'm not a prostitute," she said as she sat down next to him on the bed.

"I know," he said, kissing her lightly.

They went through all the preliminaries and everything went fine, but when they approached the main event he realized he was not going to be able to do it.

"What's wrong, Johnny?" she asked with concern.

"I can't do it. I'm a married man," he said, but that wasn't the real reason. He wanted Carolyn Broom and only Carolyn and nobody else was going to do.

The black-haired, doe-eyed girl left, and Johnny settled back to sleep. He knew he would have to have Carolyn somehow, he didn't know how. But he knew he had to have her, Willis be damned, Sarah and the kids be damned. He would figure out a way to get her.

At home, Sarah had just awakened. She got up off the couch and turned the radio off. Johnny, Jr. and Laura Mae and Cindy were asleep in different parts of the house.

"Get up and let's go to bed," she said to each of them as she shook them awake.

They each got up and pulled off their clothes and went to bed in their drawer-tails.

Sarah went around and locked the doors. She left the windows open for fresh air. The night was cool, as always.

She wondered if Johnny was asleep already. It was near midnight and the radio had been sputtering static when she turned it off. She looked through the window at the full moon and wished Johnny were with her. She hurt in the pit of her stomach. It would be easier to hurt if Johnny were here. If only I didn't have to hurt alone, she thought.

Even at midnight the trees whispered together. They heard the weeping of poor Sarah Bryson. And they felt sorrow for what awaited Johnny.

CHAPTER NINE

Ansel looked up at the huge clock on the wall of the control room. It said three-thirty. The screen door opened and a balding, short man in a white shirt and tie and the pants to an expensive suit came in. He smiled, a bit lamely.

"Hello, Ansel," he said. "Everything okay?"

"Fine, Mr. Cal," Ansel said. Ansel had always called him mister, though his name was Paul. It was because he was older and he was the boss. Turner always called him Paul.

"Who comes in today at four?" Mr. Cal asked.

"Ralph Turner," Ansel replied. "I'd better start the hourly readings."

"No, no. Let Turner get them when he comes in. They're supposed to be done every hour, on the hour. That way the men in Raleigh can tell where the power is going."

"Oh. Okay," Ansel said, and sat back down.

"You've been here for six years, Ansel. How do you like it back in here?"

"Well, you've been here seventeen years. How do you like it?"

They both laughed.

"No, I mean it, Ansel. After this thing with Broom, wouldn't you like to get out of here?"

"Now that you mention it, Mr. Cal, Alice has been nagging at me to get a transfer over to Asheville, where her people are. You reckon there's any chance of that?"

"If you want me to I'll see what I can do. You're from Alabama originally, aren't you?"

"That's right. Near Huntsville."

"Boy, that place has boomed. They're building bombs there now. Atomic bombs. Have you applied there?"

"I haven't applied anywhere. I've never applied for a job."

"I remember. You just showed up here one day. You were still working with the Civilian Conservation Corps then, weren't you?"

"Yes. I figured I'd better get something more permanent. I knew Roosevelt wouldn't be president forever, and the CCC would play out."

"You've been a good employee, Ansel. I'll see what I can do. Have you had any trouble with Broom lately?"

"He caught me one night last week. He knocked me down. He was carrying his gun, so I didn't fight him."

"I can understand that. If you stay here, Ansel, you'll have to kill him sooner or later. Or he'll kill you. He's a crazy man. My jawbone will never be the same. I could have given him a hard time twenty years ago. But now ... well, I'd call the law on him now, if we had any goddamned law."

"He'll never forgive me for telling you about his drinking. And he'll never forgive you for firing him."

"I don't give a shit if he forgives me. Look here. The old man pulled a tiny automatic pistol out of his floppy trousers. "Couldn't tell I had it, could you?"

"No. What kind is it?"

"It's a Beretta .25. Made in Italy. Maybe you ought to get one, too."

Ansel went to the back room and brought back his lunch box. He opened it and drew out the P.38.

"That would stop a horse. That's a Walther P.38, right? A German gun."

"That's right. Got it at a pawn shop in Asheville. I hope I never have to use it. Is there any accuracy to that little gun of yours?"

"Not much. He'd have to be right on top of me. But I think it's you he wants, not me."

"I think you're right."

They heard the sound of a car driving onto the gravel parking lot beside the switchyard.

"Turner, coming in five minutes early," Mr. Cal said. "That's a change. He's usually five minutes late."

"Turner's a good man," Ansel said. "He's real intelligent."

"He sure is. Well educated. He reads all the time. He's going to waste back in these woods. I hear his wife is a good piano player. She plays in one of the Newport churches. They're a fine family. They have two boys in school, I guess you know. Very smart kids, I hear. High IQ's."

"Turner's real smart. I guess he'd never carry a gun."

"Probably not," Mr. Cal said. A few moments later Turner came into the plant. He had a book under his arm which he tried to hide from Mr. Cal.

"Too late," Mr. Cal laughed. "I've already seen it, Harvey. What's the name of it?"

"It's a Russian book called *The Idiot*. It's by Dostoyevsky."

Mr. Cal and Ansel looked at each other and laughed. Turner blushed and laid the book on his desk beside the telephone.

"Let's let Turner take over and go shoot a game of pool, what do you say?" Mr. Cal said to Ansel.

"Sure thing," Ansel said. He closed his lunch box and set it back on the shelf above the desk. He followed Mr. Cal out to the game room.

"You know, Ansel, I had high hopes for you when you came here. I hoped you might take my place as plant manager. You're smart and you're dependable. I'd hate to see a dumb son-of-a-bitch like Willis Broom run you off from a good thing. Think it over for a few days and if you still feel the same, I'll process your request for a transfer."

Ansel walked out into the heat of the switchyard with his lunch box. He looked at his watch. It was four-thirty. Alice would be starting dinner.

Plant manager! He would make a lot more money at that. He had come in as relief dispatcher at two thousand a year, right before the war. He had been deferred from the draft because of the nature of his job. It was called essential. And it was, now. In the years before the plant had been built the people in this part of the mountains hadn't had any electricity at all. No radios, no refrigerators, no electric kitchen ranges. They had cooked on wood stoves and cured their meat in smokehouses and used ice-boxes.

But now it was 1950. The war was over, electricity was commonplace. Jody would never know what hard times were, Ansel thought. At least he hoped and prayed he didn't. Not like it was for him in Alabama in the twenties and thirties.

God, Ansel thought, as he recalled a picture in his memory, of his mother and his sisters and him working in the cotton fields. And the days were not eight hours long, as they were for him now. They lasted from sunup to sundown, sixteen hours at least, with a little time off to eat some collards and fatback and fritter cakes.

The thought of fritter cakes made him think of Alice's cornbread. Cornbread was surely Alice's specialty. It had been noon when he ate the two sandwiches, one bologna and one peanut butter and jelly, that Alice had fixed him that morning and placed in his lunch box on top of the gun.

The thought of the gun reminded Ansel of the bitter present. If he kills me, who'll take over when Mr. Cal dies? Turner? Turner was too smart. Book smart. He could never be a boss of other men. Ansel liked Turner, because Turner was good to talk to. He was so well-read. He was shy, too, but that was a hell of a lot better than some. Like Willis Broom. Willis was outgoing, you could say.

He walked across the swinging bridge to the sidewalk that led up to the steps up to the house. He had counted them twice. Once they came to ninety-nine and once to a hundred. Some day I'll count them again, he thought. But not today.

Plant manager. I couldn't really be plant manager, he thought. Not in a million years.

He had lied on his application form about graduating from Eufala High School. Alice had graduated from Asheville High School, but Ansel only went to the sixth grade. If they ever find it out on me they'd fire me, Ansel thought. I wouldn't even be a dispatcher.

He got to the top of the steps and Jody looked up from his play. He was riding his dog Duffy around in his wagon, singing Gene Autry songs to her. Jody ran to Ansel and Ansel held out his arms and Jody jumped up into them. Ansel carried him into the house. He could smell the cornbread cooking.

"I'm home!" he shouted. Alice came out of the kitchen wiping her hands on a hand towel. She reached up to kiss him. He was taller than she was by almost a foot.

They sat down to eat and Ansel said a quick blessing and then reached for the chicken and dumplings.

"I spoke to Mr. Cal about the transfer," Ansel said. "He said he'd help. But he wants me here to take over when he's gone, so he won't press very hard for it, I guess. I'm sorry, Alice."

Alice looked down. "I guess it can't be helped. But I do wish we could leave here, Ansel. Will you talk to him again and make him understand about it? He knows about Willis and you, doesn't he?"

"Willis put him in the hospital. And he knows Willis hates me. But I'm afraid it'll come to a head before I ever get a transfer, even if I get one. And he could come over the mountain. It's not that far."

"Ansel, that's not the only reason I want us to get out of here. There's Jody. He can't get decent schooling in that little one-room schoolhouse up on Mt. Sterling. And it would be so nice to live in a nice town..."

"That's enough! That's all I want to hear!" Ansel said, putting down his fork. "Every day you nag me about it. I'm doing the best I can. I've spoken to Mr. Cal about it. That's all I can do."

"Okay," Alice said, getting up from the table. She went to the bedroom and lay down on the bed and put her face in the pillow and wept softly.

Ansel knew what she was doing and so did Jody. Jody didn't like his father when he made his mother cry.

At this time of year the leaves were changing their colors, from green to gold and yellow and brown and red, a celebration of life and death. The trees were at their peak of splendor as autumn came to the Great Smoky Mountains.

CHAPTER TEN

Willis sat brooding in his big chair, listening to "Howdy Doody" and drinking a beer. Carolyn was in the kitchen fixing supper. He was angry. Angry at Ansel Harper, angry at Johnny Bryson. He would have to decide which one he would get even with first. He had seen how Johnny looked at Carolyn. His brain began to work on a plan. He knew Johnny was saving his money. Everybody knew it, because Johnny was always talking about it. He was saving cash, not in the bank but carrying it with him.

"Carolyn!" he called out. "Come here a minute, doll."

"What you want, Willis? I've just about got supper on the table." She walked into the living room from the kitchen.

"How would you like us to lay our hands on a cool thousand dollars?"

"I'd like it fine. But how?"

"Have you ever noticed how Johnny looks at you when he thinks I'm not looking?"

"He likes me, I guess."

"He'd do anything you asked him to."

"What are you driving at, Willis?"

"That boy has close to a thousand on him, Carolyn. You could get him to turn it loose long enough for me to get my hands on it. That's all. It would be real easy."

"You must be crazy, Willis," she laughed.

Willis hit her in the stomach with his fist. She doubled up and fell on the couch, gasping.

"I've asked you nicely. Now I'm telling you. Johnny will be coming over tomorrow to get a big load of whiskey to take to Asheville. I'll tell him that he can drop off my money the next day, but I'll be gone all day that day, but he can leave the money with you."

"But ... how will you ... get the money ... away from him?" Carolyn gasped.

"You just do your part and let me worry about the rest of it."

"Okay, Willis," Carolyn said. "I'll do it if you want me to."

"Now let's eat," Willis said.

It was also suppertime at the Harper home. Alice was making meat loaf. She kneaded the ground steak and the bits of bread and the ketchup all together and put the whole blob in the oven.

"What's for supper?" Ansel hollered from the living room.

"Meat loaf," Alice said. "Like your mother used to make. She gave me her recipe."

"I get a little tired of meat loaf," Ansel said weakly.

"You get tired? You get tired? How tired do you think I get? You whine just like a little boy. Damn!"

"You shouldn't curse, Alice. That sounds bad coming from a woman."

At that Alice laughed and sat down in Ansel's lap.

"You want to let supper wait a few minutes, Sweetheart?" Alice asked.

"Yeah," Ansel said, and they went off to the bedroom.

"Jody's out in the back yard playing with Duffy. Do you want us to lock the door?"

"Yes," Ansel said.

In a few minutes they opened the door and Jody had been looking through the key hole.

Alice and Ansel were embarrassed. Jody didn't know why. He couldn't see anything through the key hole anyway. He supposed they were talking adult stuff not for his ears.

"Jody, your mommy and I need our privacy sometimes. Do you know what privacy means?" Ansel asked.

"No, Daddy," Jody said.

"It means when you want to do something that's nobody else's business but your own, and you want to be left alone. Like when you're reading a funny book."

The thought of comics cheered Jody up. He loved comics: Uncle Scrooge, Black Rider, Superman.

Ansel sent Jody to wash up for supper.

Jody loved his daddy, but sometimes he was afraid of him. He would sometimes pull off his belt and whip Jody. Ansel was a young man and really didn't know much about how to raise children. He and Alice did the best they could. "Spare not the rod to spoil the child," Ansel said now and again, and "As the twig is bent, so grows the tree." All Jody knew was that these sayings meant he should be whipped sometimes.

Ansel himself had been whipped when he was a child, sometimes unmercifully, by a drunken father. Ansel hardly ever drank. He kept a bottle of Seagram's Seven in the pantry for medicinal purposes. And it really was for medicinal purposes: when one of them got a cough, he would mix some sugar with the whiskey to make a cough syrup.

All in all, Ansel was not a bad father. He always had time to talk to Jody, Alice thought. Alice never whipped Jody. She always left that to Ansel, because he was the man of the family.

They sat down to supper. Jody said the blessing and they ate in silence. Whatever it was they were doing, it made them sweat, Jody thought.

Down the road toward Newport, Johnny and Sarah sat down to supper with Johnny, Jr., Laura Mae, and Cindy. They said no blessing.

"Pass the corn," Johnny said to Sarah.

"Johnny, I want to talk to you. I wish you wouldn't run any more whiskey."

"Pass the corn," Johnny said. "You know that's like askin' me to quit breathing, Sarah Jo."

He called her "Sarah Jo" when he was being patronizing. It made Sarah angry.

"You're gonna get killed messing with that stuff. You know it's against the law. Some police or state trooper is going to kill you – shoot you or run you off the road. Why don't you quit it, Johnny? Please?"

"That's how I made the money I got saved up, Sarah Jo. Maybe I could make it working on cars if I had my own garage. But that would cost me close to ten thousand dollars."

"You could go in debt for it, and use the thousand you got as a down payment."

"We already got a mortgage payment of fifty dollars a month. And the power bill and the food bill and the telephone bill. I got to have steady money, real money, coming in. And I get it from running whiskey. And I play a good game of poker. I can pick up a few hundred a month at that."

"None of that is steady, Johnny. A garage would be steady and it would be honest work, with no risk to your life. Why don't you, Honey?"

"Okay. I'll think about it. But I don't like the idea of going that deep in debt."

As they were finishing supper, the phone rang and Johnny answered it.

"Hello, Johnny," Willis said. "I need you to run me another load over to Asheville tomorrow. Can you come by here tomorrow evening about 5:00? I'll have the stuff boxed up and ready to go."

"I'll be there," Johnny said. "How much you want for it?"

"Five hundred. I'll give you fifty."

"Sounds good."

"See you tomorrow," Willis said.

"So long," Johnny said, hanging up the phone.

"Was that Willis, Honey?" Sarah asked.

"Yes. One more load and then maybe I'll try something else."

"Oh, Johnny, that would be so nice."

"Don't get your hopes up too high, Sarah. You know that running whiskey is something I'm good at."

"You're good at working on cars, too, Johnny. I'm sure you'd make a success of it."

"Maybe after this load. We'll see," Johnny said.

Sarah took the supper dishes to the kitchen. Johnny went into the living room, to his favorite chair. He lit a cigarette and thought of Carolyn.

The trees that cast their giant shadows over the little village of Waterville looked down upon the human beings there. They sensed the love among the Harpers and the dog, Duffy; and they also felt the meanness of the monster Broom and the sorrow of his woman Carolyn and of poor Johnny and Sarah. Humans were a pitiful race, the trees whispered and nodded.

CHAPTER ELEVEN

Alice had decided what she had to do. She had to help Ansel somehow, and so she had to have a friend, a friend with pull. She would use that pull to get Ansel a transfer to the Asheville plant.

Everything would be so much better in Asheville, she thought as she ironed out her best dress. Asheville was a big town with places to go and things to do. Ansel would make better money and she could shop during the day while Jody was in school or she could just sit sometimes and listen to the radio.

The radio was on and Lefty Frizzell was singing "Always Late." She remembered how she used to be late to school on pretty spring days when she would stop and smell the camelias and the lovely honeysuckle on the way. Her sisters would call to her to come on but she always tarried. Life then was so good, so sweet. She was poor then but she didn't realize it. She had nobody rich to compare herself to. Not at least until the high school prom. She would never forget that the rest of her life.

Buddy Rogers had invited her to the dance and then he came by in his father's truck, two days before the dance, and told her he couldn't take her. He didn't think she'd go at all but her mother had sewn her a gown, an Alice blue gown, like the song, so she went with some girl friends who were also poor but who were also fat and unattractive.

Then at the dance she saw Buddy. He was dancing with Roberta Bryson and she found out he had brought Roberta to the dance. Roberta was Dr. Bryson's daughter, and they were very well-to-do. She knew Buddy liked her but it wasn't enough. She wasn't good enough for him.

She had not felt that old hurt often in the last seven years since she had been married to Ansel. She had always thought Ansel was the best-looking man she had ever seen. He was poor, too. He was in the CCC when she met him. They were paving a sidewalk right down the road from her house and when she came home from school those warm spring days when they first met she would see him working, his muscles glistening with sweat, and he would look up from mixing the concrete and look at her and smile. His teeth were blazing, faultless white and she would think about him at night in bed before she went to sleep. He had always made her feel so special, so loved, without them exchanging a word. He could be hateful sometimes but he was good to her and Jody most of the time.

She finished ironing the dress and then she stepped out of her house dress and put the fresh one on. It was the dress she had worn to the dance. She looked at herself in the big mirror on the bathroom door and buttoned the dress up. She had to strain to get the buttons up the back but finally it was all buttoned up and it looked fine.

"Jody!" she hollered out the back door. Jody was playing with Duffy in the yard between their house and the Milsaps'. "Come in here and bring Duffy with you."

He came running.

"We're going down to the Mundy's house. Will you be nice?"

"Okay, Mommy," Jody said gleefully.

They walked down the hundred steps to the sidewalk and then down the sidewalk a mile, beside the river and past the swinging bridge to the Mundy's house. It was the last house in the village, and the nicest and cleanest. Alice was nervous as she pressed the doorbell.

Sylvia opened the door. Sylvia was thirty-five but was very tan and looked as if she were in her twenties. She had on bright red lipstick and had her hair tied back with a black scarf. She had an electric vacuum cleaner behind her and was obviously cleaning house. She even looked stylish in her work clothes, a black sleeveless top and white pedal-pushers.

"Come in, Alice and Jody! I haven't seen you all for months. Alice, would you like some coffee?"

"Yes, thank you," Alice said. "I need to talk to you."

"That's fine. What about?"

"Well, I ...," Alice stammered.

"First, let me get our coffee. I need a cup myself." "Well," Sylvia said when they sat down on the living room sofa, a rich, plush green thing. "How nice you look."

"I've had this for years."

They sat and looked at each other for a long moment. "Did you have something you want to talk to me about, Alice?" Sylvia asked with a polite but curious smile.

"Here, Jody, you look at these funny books while we talk."

"Well, yes," Alice said. "You must know about this trouble Ansel is having with Willis Broom ..."

"I've heard about it, yes. Will told me about it. It seems Ansel reported Willis for being drunk on the job and Mr. Cal fired him. He broke Mr. Cal's jaw and put him in the hospital for two weeks. I guess everyone knows that."

"There's more, Sylvia. Willis has been threatening Ansel. He's even threatened me and Jody. He's so wild and mean, I'm scared of him. I want Ansel to get a transfer."

"Well, I can understand that. But I don't see why ..."

"I came to you because you might have some influence on Kelly. He's area supervisor and all ... and I know you and he are ... friends."

Sylvia's face turned pale and she set her coffee cup and saucer down on the expensive coffee table.

"Just what have you heard about Mr. Kelly and me, Alice?" Sylvia asked with her curious smile. Alice knew she had made a mistake.

"Nothing. I just know he's friends with you and Will."

"We're all good friends. Bob Kelly and Patricia and Will and me."

"Of course. That's all I meant. I want Ansel to get us out of here. I don't want a show-down between them. I hoped you might understand and ask Mr. Kelly, or ask Will to ask him to help Ansel get a transfer over to Asheville."

"Your family is from Asheville, aren't they, Alice?" Sylvia asked.

"Yes. It's just Mama, now, and my three younger sisters. I haven't been back since Daddy's funeral last year. I'd like to be closer to them. They could help me with Jody and Asheville is a big town with lots of nice things to do and ... I guess I'm just boring you."

"Not at all. Asheville is a nice town. And I know what you mean. A woman needs to get away from the kids now and then. Thank goodness Jesse is old enough now to take care of himself pretty much. But we're so far back in here that I get so bored. I guess that's why, we've grown so close to Bob and Patricia. They have new things to tell us. You know they went to Mexico last summer and they're going to Hawaii this year. They're always going places and doing things. Their two girls are grown, though they're still at home. They're so ugly they'll never marry, I suspect. They take after Patricia. Now I'm talking too much."

They both laughed.

Sylvia sipped her coffee and looked hard at Alice. She set the cup down slowly.

"You think there's something between me and Bob Kelly, I guess.

Alice shook her head, lying. "Oh, no. If there is, it would be your business and nobody else's, Sylvia.

Sylvia got up and took their coffee cups into the kitchen.

"More coffee, Alice?" Sylvia asked over her shoulder.

"Oh, no. No. thanks. I've got to be going."

Sylvia came back into the living room. Alice was standing and Sylvia clasped Alice's hands in hers.

"Don't worry. I'll say something to Bob about Ansel. We can't have one of our handsomest young men killed off by a stupid hillbilly like Willis Broom, can we?"

"Thank you Sylvia. Jody, it's time to go."

Sylvia smiled her best smile, with perfect white teeth and dimples in her cheeks. There were little wrinkles around her eyes. Alice thought she would like to look like her when she got to be forty.

Alice and Jody walked the long way up the sidewalk, past the other houses of Waterville Village and to the swinging bridge and then up the steps to the Harper house. The sun told her she had better start dinner, for Ansel would be home soon.

Nearby trees overheard the mention of the name of the monster Broom, and shuddered all around the little village. The monster Broom meant death and sorrow for the poor humans. The humans' lives were so short compared to those of the trees, and they seemed compelled to try to kill one another anyway. They were pitiful creatures.

CHAPTER TWELVE

"Johnny should be here about two o'clock," Willis said. "That's when he usually comes over. Have you got it straight what you're supposed to do?"

"After I get your whiskey money then I get him into the bedroom. Right?"

"Right. You just get him in the bedroom and leave the rest up to me. And don't mess this up. If you do I'll whip you like you've never been whipped before."

Willis went out to the still and Carolyn turned on the radio and tried to fix the house up and clean it a little. It was a hopeless mess, really, Carolyn thought. Willis was nasty as a hog. He tromped in with his old muddy shoes and threw his dirty clothes all around. Beer cans and cigarette butts were all around his favorite chair. She didn't have much heart to clean the house up. Why bother, she thought.

The day went by slowly for Carolyn and Willis and Johnny and Sarah. When Johnny got up, after he'd had his first cup of coffee, Sarah decided to tell him about her sickness.

"I'm sick, Johnny. I'm afraid it's something bad. I need to go to Newport to see Dr. Mears. Will you take me this afternoon if I call him, Johnny?"

"I've got something to do this afternoon, Sarah. Urgent business. I'll be back by four o'clock. Will the doctor be in that late?" Johnny asked.

"I'll ask him. Thanks, Honey," she said. "What kind of business have you got?"

"I've got to go see Willis and take him his whiskey money," he said.

"Are you running more moonshine for him, Johnny?" Sarah asked. "I thought you were quitting that."

"Naw, naw. It ain't moonshine."

"What, then?"

"I got to go out for awhile, Sarah Jo. I'll see you directly."

Johnny got into his Ford and drove around awhile. He was on pins and needles. He could hardly wait to get to Carolyn. He drove to Newport and shot pool until about one-thirty. He figured Willis would be gone by that time. When he got to Willis's house, he was pleased to see Willis's truck was nowhere to be seen.

"Carolyn?" Johnny said softly as he pulled open the screen door of Willis's house.

"Come on in, Johnny."

"Hello, Carolyn," Johnny said, his mouth dry.

"Hello, Johnny. Willis ain't here."

"Yeah, that's what he said yesterday. He said I could leave his whiskey money with you."

He felt afire with wanting her. She looked at him. She could tell he was excited and that excited her, too. Both were in the grip of guilty passion, the sweetest and most terrible emotion that human beings ever feel.

"I like your house," he said. "It's nice. Can you show me the bedroom?" His mouth was so dry he could hardly speak and his heart was pounding with fear and passion.

"Okay," she said. She took his hand and led him into the bedroom. He pulled her to him and kissed her on the mouth, softly. She kissed him back, hard. She began squirming and rubbing herself on him.

He moved his hands up her dress and pulled her panties down and they both sat on the bed and she kicked her panties off. He rubbed her under her dress and kept kissing her. She unbuckled his belt and zipped down his pants and held him. She lay back on the bed.

Johnny had plunged into her three or four times when she screamed. What the hell? he wondered. She was looking over his shoulder toward the bedroom door. He stopped and looked around, hearing two clicks as he turned. He saw Willis and the shotgun for a second. Then both barrels went off and blew his head away. He fell back on Carolyn and was dead.

Carolyn jumped screaming from the bed and ran to the window she had left open and scrambled through it and ran into the woods.

Willis grabbed Johnny's jeans and got his wallet. He grinned as he reloaded his shotgun and put it back into the bedroom closet. He got a shovel from the back porch and took the money to the big maple tree and buried it.

You're next, Ansel Harper, Willis said to himself. Willis Broom pays his debts.

The explosion of the double-barreled shotgun made the whole forest tremble – the trees, the animals, every living thing paused, all the way from Mt. Sterling to Walters Dam. The blast caused a ripple of many colors throughout the whole forest.

CHAPTER THIRTEEN

The trial was expected to last for a week or two. Sheriff Pete Broom went back to his brother's cell and rapped his billy stick on the bars.

"Go to hell, big brother," Willis snarled.

"I'm coming in to talk to you a spell, Willis," Pete said. "So just relax and act nice or I'll forget you're my little brother and I'll bounce this goddamned blackjack off your stupid head."

"You got no right to call me stupid. Get out of here."

"I got a question or two to ask you. Did you know Carolyn's run off?"

"Where to?" Willis asked, his eyebrows raised.

"Folks say she's staying with her people in Newport."

"That won't last too long. Her daddy's in his second childhood."

"You've talked to Lawyer Donley, I guess. How's he going to defend you?"

"Justifiable homicide. I come in and find a man screwing my wife, I go crazy and run and get the shotgun and come back and kill him. That's how it was, and so I'll plead innocent. I'll get out of here in a week or two."

"You made it look real good, Willis, by calling me. But there's a detail or two we got to clear up. Like what went with Johnny's money?"

"Money? What money?" Willis's eyes grew large.

"Don't try to fool me, Willis. I know you. Johnny had about a thousand dollars saved up. You got it. Or at least Johnny's wife Sarah says you did."

"Did she see me get it?"

"It'd be bad for you if that money turned up, wouldn't it, Willis? It's part of my job to try to find it. And I think I know just where to look."

"Don't you go poking around my house," Willis said, standing up, his fists clenched.

"Don't be so loud. There's other prisoners in here, too. If I find it, it'll be mine," Pete said. "I won't say a word about it."

Pete chuckled as he turned to go.

"If you do, Pete, when I get out I'll whip you."

"I'm surprised you didn't say you'd kill me. You're getting good at killing. There was that salesman from New Jersey, and Johnny ..."

"I've never killed nobody. Nobody. I'll whip you for that, Pete." Willis sat back down on his cot.

"You're going to start believing you can get away with anything, Willis. That's dangerous. You'll wind up either dead or in prison for a long time. And you wouldn't last a month in prison. You don't give. You got to give some in life, little brother. Bend a little."

Pete opened the jail door and stepped out, locking it behind him.

Willis looked at him. "If you touch that money I'll whip you, big brother. I mean it. Sheriff or not."

Pete grinned and left. He went out to his car and sped out of the dirt parking lot onto the blacktop and headed over Cataloochee. He figured that he knew pretty well where Willis hid the money. When they were kids on Red Dog Willis had stolen a pocket knife at the hardware store in Newport. It was a treasure, he told Pete, and he was going to bury it like buried treasure in the stories they had heard in school. That was the only kind of story Willis ever learned or cared about. Pirate treasure.

The blacktop turned to dirt halfway up the road from Waynesville to Cataloochee. It was a trip Pete had made many times over to Waterville Village and Red Dog and Newport. He slowed down from sixty to forty and the Ford still slid in the curves. It took an hour to get across Cataloochee. The name, his grandfather had told him many years before, meant "up close to God". It was a Cherokee name. Pete's grandfather had lived with a Cherokee woman so Pete guessed the old man must have known what he was talking about. Pete didn't feel close to God as he drove over the top of Cataloochee and down toward Tennessee. He felt close to money. And the closer he got to Red Dog, the stronger he felt it.

He pulled the Ford up into Willis's yard. Nobody was around so he got out and walked past the house to the back yard. He looked at the patch on the roof. He and Willis had put that patch there themselves, fifteen years before. A big windstorm, some said it was a tornado, had come through and knocked a few trees down and one had fallen on the roof and punched a hole through it. Pete and Willis got drunk and bought some poorly matched shingles and climbed up on the roof and nailed them down. Willis fell off, laughing and acting a fool, and broke his hand. He was still laughing when Pete drove him to Dr. Mears's Clinic in Newport.

Their Mama was alive then, and it was before the war. Pete served his two years but when Willis volunteered they wouldn't take him. Pete had always wondered why. At the time Willis volunteered they were taking almost everybody but they didn't take Willis because he was the only boy left at home. At least that was the way Willis told it. Pete often had thought it might have been because Willis was so mean and crazy.

They had sent Tommy to North Africa and Pete to the South Pacific. The patch in the roof brought all the old memories back. It was enough to make you cry, Pete thought.

He went and looked under the big old maple tree and there was the fresh dirt. He dug down with his hands about a foot and there was the paper bag. Pete grinned to himself. Willis had pulled off a good one this time. It was too bad he had to kill somebody to get it, but you can't always have everything the way you want it. Pete opened the bag to count the money and to his horror there were only five twenty dollar bills and the rest was old scraps of newspaper. Where was the thousand dollars?

He put the twenties down in his trousers pocket and went back to his police car.

Pete pulled his car up in the yard of the Bryson house and got out. He went up onto the porch and knocked on the door.

Sarah Bryson answered the door. The three children trailed along behind her, Johnny, Jr. with a thumb in his mouth. She looked worn out, with dark bags under her eyes. She looked as if she weighed eighty pounds.

"Hello, Sheriff," she said, "come on in the house. It's dirty and I apologize but I ain't had time to clean it up none since Johnny got killed."

"I just dropped by to see how you were making out. It's a sad thing to happen to you and the kids. Are you eating good? You look a little peaked."

"We're all okay, Sheriff, thank you. We're low on money, that's for sure. Something went with the money Johnny had saved, you know."

"Johnny was wrong to be messing with, somebody else's wife, Sarah. You know that."

"Yes," she said, and looked down, ashamed.

"Well, I've come to help you out some. Here's forty dollars to help out with food for you and the kids."

Sarah took the money and thanked Pete and Pete left.

Willis paced back and forth in the Haywood County jail. He knew where Pete had gone and what he was doing. He swore at himself under his breath for being so stupid as to hide the money in the one place Pete would find it. Pete had never forgotten that goddamn pocket knife and the big old maple tree.

"Shit," he said, and sat down. Deputy Lamarr, one of the two deputies who worked for Pete, came back to check on him.

"What did you say, Willis? Is there something I can get for you?"

"Go screw yourself," Willis growled.

"No need to get upset, Willis. You know you might not get out of this one."

"Go on and leave me alone," Willis said. "It'll be a cold day in hell before they put me in a damn state pen."

The trees sensed the sheriff walking to his car and they heard the muffled crying of the woman in the house. They knew human beings were capable of senseless cruelty, especially, it seemed, to those they were supposed to love and care about.

They felt this troubled time was not yet over and would not be over until the monster Broom and his awful brother were gone.

CHAPTER FOURTEEN

Fall was turning the green mountain leaves to red, gold, yellow and brown. There had been enough rain to produce a blaze of color in the thick foliage. The woods were more beautiful than they had been in years.

Alice and Ansel sat at the kitchen table over eggs and bacon and cream of wheat and coffee.

"Are you going to the trial? It should be the last day of it today," Alice said.

"Yes, I guess I will. Want to come with me?"

"God, no!" Alice said. "I don't want anywhere around that Willis Broom. You think they'll turn him loose?"

"The sheriff who has him locked up is Willis's brother. The judge is distantly related to him. The jury was picked so that none of them know him. All that's in Willis's favor."

"But Sarah Bryson testified that her husband took a lot of money with him, and it was never found," Alice said.

"But why didn't he shoot Carolyn, too, if he was in a fit of jealous rage, the way the lawyer is making out?" Ansel said.

"I'll bet you anything that Willis set Johnny up to kill him and take his money."

"Johnny should never have kept that much money with him. He should have put it in the bank," Ansel said. "He went around talking about it to everybody. Everybody knew he had it. But it was dirty money, made from moonshine whiskey."

"It's an awful thing to die and leave a wife and three little kids. How old is little Cindy? No more than three. How awful to leave them with no daddy. And have you noticed how sickly looking Sarah is," Alice said to Ansel. "She looks like she's got something bad."

"They were so poor and nasty, it might be something like tuberculosis," Ansel said.

They finished breakfast and then Jody got up.

"Listen, why don't we all go and see the end of the trial?" Ansel suggested.

"Do they let little kids in?" Alice asked.

"I reckon so. I read in the paper where Sarah and the kids sat in on the trial the last day or so."

"I'm afraid to go, Ansel. What if they turn him loose? He'll be after you next."

"Aw," come on and go. Maybe they'll put him in jail the rest of his life. I'd like to see that."

"Me, too. Okay, then, we'll go."

While Ansel and Alice and Jody were dressing to go, Sarah was trying to get the kids ready. She wanted them to look clean and nice. The prosecutor had told her it would help convict Willis. Sarah was in pain. The soreness and ache in her stomach had grown to a throbbing torture. She almost didn't care whether Willis was convicted or not. Soon the kids would be without anybody.

She planned to give the kids to her sister. She had two of her own and she wasn't well off, but her husband was a good man. They'd take care of them, she was sure. All that was left was to die. She didn't know how, but she figured she would have to. Her father had always told her not to whine. That was the only good advice he ever gave her, but it would come in handy now. She had decided she would die in silence, without whining.

Carolyn was in the bathroom at her folks' house in Newport getting ready to go to the last day of the trial. She had not been asked to testify by either side.

It was if she didn't exist, didn't matter. Why? she asked herself. Why should she go to the trial? She didn't give a damn what became of Willis.

She pulled her dress on over her head but she left her shoes off and lay down on the living room couch, and there she stayed.

Ansel and Alice and Jody sat in the courtroom, listening to the prosecution sum up their case:

"Ladies and gentlemen of the jury," the district attorney, David Frye, was saying, "we have here all the evidence we need to return a verdict of guilty in the first degree. It is clear, beyond the shadow of a reasonable doubt, that Willis Broom killed Johnny Bryson. Willis admits that much. But furthermore he killed Johnny with premeditation. In other words, ladies and gentlemen, it was planned. The motive was the thousand dollars that Johnny's wife Sarah has told us about. That was murder."

"Look at her, sitting here in this courtroom, with her helpless and now fatherless children, little Johnny, Jr., and Laura Mae, and poor little Cindy. Can you see the enormity of this murder, what Willis has done?"

"Willis did it, and he did it with malice aforethought. He planned it. Why have they not brought Carolyn Broom, Willis's wife, to testify? Because even she would not be able to hold a straight face and look us in the eye and say it wasn't planned. She knew it was planned because she was in on it. She helped by luring poor Johnny to his death. And he came to her with his life's savings, just to impress her. Willis lay in wait, hiding somewhere outside the house, and when Johnny and Carolyn were in bed, he brought in his shotgun and murdered Johnny."

"And that is murder in the first degree, ladies and gentlemen. For that, Willis Broom should get the death penalty, or at the very least life imprisonment. You cannot allow a man as dangerous as he is to walk out of here a free man! He is guilty, guilty, guilty!"

Then the defense attorney, Mr. Rupert Donley, addressed the jury:

"Ladies and gentlemen of the jury, we have before us a clear and simple example of a killing done in the heat of passion, of jealous outrage. Mr. Broom came into his house and found his wife, whom he loved dearly and with whom he had lived ten years, locked in sexual embrace with Johnny Bryson. He was wild with anger as he went automatically to the closet and took out his shot-gun and impulsively shot Johnny Bryson, a young man who had no respect for marriage vows, his own or anyone else's.

"You cannot in good conscience find Willis Broom guilty of premeditated murder, of murder in the first degree. And he is not charged with second degree murder, but with first degree murder. Premeditated murder. And he is clearly innocent of that. That's all, your honor, and ladies and gentlemen of the jury."

The jury retired to consider its verdict. In the courtroom sat many employees of the power company, including Ansel Harper. Alice was there, too, and Jody, and friends and neighbors of both Willis and Johnny. Ray Moore and Jeff Spence were there, as were Sarah and her three children.

It didn't matter much to Sarah. Part of her wanted revenge, and the other part didn't care. The money was gone and the pictures taken by the police photographer showed clearly that Johnny had his pants down, so she knew that it was a set-up that Johnny had stupidly stumbled into. She felt more anger and resentment toward Johnny than she did toward Willis. Still she hoped justice would prevail.

Ansel and Alice and Jody, of course, all hoped Willis would be found guilty. It would make life easier for them.

Ray and Jeff didn't give a damn one way or the other. It would tickle them for Willis to go to jail for life, and it would tickle them if he were turned loose on the public.

Most of the people in the courtroom walked outside to wait for the jury to come back. In a very short few minutes the jury did just that.

"Your honor," the foreman said, "we find the defendant, Willis Broom, not guilty of murder in the first degree."

Willis jumped up and hollered and laughed. Ray and Jeff cheered. Carolyn was not in the courtroom. She couldn't testify against Willis, and the defense attorney decided she was too slow to help as a defense witness. It was a smart move, because she had already decided, in her clouded and confused way, to tell the truth about it.

She had run away that day into the woods. Willis had called the sheriff, his brother, himself. A deputy had found Carolyn huddled in the shadow of a balsam tree in a clearing in the woods the next day.

Ansel and Alice and Jody left without congratulating Willis. Once outside in the cool autumn sun they looked at each other.

"So he's still loose," Alice said.

"Yes, and now he knows he can get away with murder," Ansel said. They went to their car and drove off toward home.

Back in the courtroom, Ray and Jeff were slapping Willis on the back and laughing.

"Well, you pulled that one off slick, Willis," Ray said.

"You got away with murder," Jeff said loudly.

Willis grabbed Jeff by the shirt. "Shut your stupid mouth."

"Ah, don't worry Willis," Jeff said. "They can't try you twice for the same crime."

"Yeah," Willis said, "just the same, shut your mouth." Willis looked around in the courtroom. He saw everyone leaving. The people looked downcast. Willis was smart enough to know what an unpopular decision it was. He grinned a big grin and slapped Ray and Jeff on the back. "I'm a free man, boys," he said.

Lawyer Donley came back and shook Willis's hand. "You were lucky, Mr. Broom. If I were you I'd stay out of trouble from now on. I managed to introduce a reasonable doubt into the jurors' minds. You might not be so lucky next time."

"Go to hell," Willis said. "I don't need you no more."

Donley turned and walked away. He was sorry to have been a part of such a blatant miscarriage of justice. Willis should be put in jail for the rest of his life, he thought.

Willis went by the sheriff"s office to pick up his belongings, including his .38. "Pete," he said in a whisper, "that money better be where I left it." Then he went out to the courthouse parking lot and got into his truck and drove away toward home.

He got to Red Dog in the early afternoon. He had missed lunch at the jail and he was hungry. He pulled up in the yard and got out. The front door was closed, and he swore under his breath.

The woods knew nothing of human laws and courthouses. But they saw Willis come out of the big building in the center of Waynesville wearing a big grin, with people shaking his hand and patting him on the back. He went to his truck and sped off over Cataloochee to Red Dog.

The trees were puzzled that the monster Broom should be set free among other humans.

CHAPTER FIFTEEN

Ansel said goodnight to Ralph Turner, who was pulling the graveyard shift, and went to his desk drawer and took out the P.38 and put it in his lunch box.

"What are you carrying that for, Ansel?" Turner asked. "Are you expecting trouble?" Turner was a civilized, educated man, a good man whom Ansel liked.

"I guess I am. Willis has threatened me and Alice. He's liable to show up drunk with that revolver he carries all the time. And since he beat that murder rap he probably thinks he can get away with anything."

"I wouldn't want to have a shootout with that Willis," Turner said. "Last year at the turkey shoot Willis won hands down. He's a good shot. And he was half drunk at the time. Does he still hold it against you that you reported him for drinking?"

"Willis never forgets anything."

Ansel went out and let the screen door of the plant slam behind him.

The sound roused Willis, who had been waiting for Ansel in the parking lot. He was completely drunk.

"Ansel!" Willis hollered. Ansel stopped and froze. He fumbled in his lunch box for the P. 38. He got it out and dropped his lunch box with a loud clatter.

"What you got there, Ansel?" Willis asked. "You got a gun? Huh? I'm not ready to kill you yet. First, I'm going to whip the shit out of you. You tattling bastard. That gun won't stop me. See, I've got one, too."

He pulled his revolver out of his pants and aimed it at Ansel. "You're too big a coward to shoot me, Ansel. You ain't got it in you." He laid his gun down on the hood of Turner's car. "I'm going to whip you, Ansel. Why don't you lay that gun down? You ain't going to use it."

Ansel laid his gun on the top of his car. Willis rushed at him. Ansel dodged and Willis went into the car door, bloodying his head. He got up and rushed Ansel again. This time he caught Ansel by the waist and they both went down on the pavement.

You can't hurt a drunk man, Ansel remembered. Better put him out of commission right away. Ansel rolled away and got up. As Willis was getting up Ansel brought his knee up hard into Willis's face. Willis fell backwards and bumped his head on the pavement and was out. Ansel stood a few moments until it looked like Willis was out for good. But then Willis came around as Ansel was walking over to his lunch box. Willis grabbed his .38 from the hood of the car and aimed it at Ansel.

"So long, bastard," Willis said, his finger tightening on the trigger.

"Hold it, Willis!" It was Turner with a shotgun, aimed at Willis. "You're going to have to fight fair this time."

"Sure," he said, laying his gun aside. "Sure thing, Turner. But I'll remember you for this."

"That's fine. You remember it," Turner said.

Willis began to circle Ansel, more wary this time. Ansel punched him with his left and then harder with his right. Willis went down again, but got back up. He rushed Ansel again and got him in a hammer-lock and started pounding him in the face.

"I'm going to kill you with my bare hands, Ansel," Willis said, and bashed Ansel's head into the fender of his car. Ansel was addled. Then he felt Willis's hands on his neck, choking him. It was all he could do to squirm out of Willis's grip. He was still down so when Willis got up he kicked Ansel in the chest as hard as he could. Ansel doubled up in pain.

Willis started dragging Ansel by the legs over to the guardrail over the tailrace. Ansel revived enough to realize that it would be certain death to be thrown into the tailrace. He kicked and Willis turned loose and fell toward the rail. Ansel got up and tried to grab Willis. Willis was hanging over the guardrail and Ansel had him by his shirt, about to shove him over.

He couldn't do it. He pulled Willis back to safe ground and hit him full in the mouth, hurting his hand. Willis staggered back and got his bearings and came at Ansel again, hitting him hard with a haymaker. Ansel stumbled back.

"You should have let me go over. You should have shot me. You're stupid, Ansel."

Ansel hit him with all his might and Willis staggered and fell. After a while he got up, got his gun from the hood of Turner's car and put it under his belt. Turner kept the shotgun trained on him the whole time.

"You'll wish you'd killed me, Ansel," Willis said, and got into his truck. "You, too piss ant," he said to Turner.

Ansel put his gun back into his lunch box.

"Maybe you should have let him fall, Ansel. It would have been just what he deserved. Come on back in the plant and wash up. You shouldn't let Alice see you that way."

"I did him some damage, too," Ansel said.

"You just made him meaner and sneakier, Ansel, that's all. You'd better really watch out from now on."

"Yeah, I guess you're right. Where'd the shotgun come from?"

"I've been carrying it in my car ever since I heard Willis was hanging around here."

Ansel washed his face but he was still bleeding when he left. He thought as he was walking up the sidewalk to the swinging bridge that all it takes is one savage person and all at once everybody is carrying a gun. He hated guns, even his own. It probably had been used to kill people during the war. Ansel never hunted and he was a poor shot. He wished he had shot Willis or let him drown in the tailrace; for now, Ansel knew, it would be a shoot out, a gunfight, to the death. How did I get into this?

He wished, as he walked across the swinging bridge, that he could just take Alice and Jody and go somewhere else, way the hell away from Waterville Village and Newport and Willis Broom.

Waterville Village, he thought, would miss him, it was such a tiny place, carved out of the deep woods by Burton Smith, a power company man who supervised the building of the dam and the community. Ansel wondered as he looked at the darkness beyond the street lights, why would Burton Smith pick such a God-forsaken place.

Ansel, like Jody, liked the dark woods of Waterville Village. Maybe, though, it's time to move on. But then I'd be running away. Away from Willis Broom.

He remembered what his father had told him about right and wrong. Always think, his father said, of what the average person would do, and do that. Ansel had given up long ago the hope of being an outstanding or special person, like Burton Smith. He would never move mountains. The best he'd be able to do was to raise Jody and keep his family fed and clothed. After the depression that seemed like quite enough.

The depression had left his family destitute. They were sharecroppers and tenant farmers in Alabama. Sometimes they had no shoes for him and his brothers and sisters. Those were hard times; 1950 was one hell of a lot better. And Ansel had done well to keep his job for so many years. He didn't intend to leave because of Willis.

He didn't want to kill Willis and he didn't want to run away. Nor did he wish to be killed himself. He seemed to have no good choices.

He started up the hundred steps. The night was chilly, typical of an October mountain night. Such a beautiful place, Ansel thought. The moon was full and Halloween was not far off. The stars became plainer as the weather grew colder. He would have to show Jody the constellation Cassiopeia, the big "W" in the night sky. There was Orion, near the eastern horizon, and the Big and Little Dippers in the west.

Ansel had heard of places which were so smoggy that you could barely see the stars. He never wanted to live in a place like that. He had also heard that in the Southern Hemisphere you saw an entirely different set of constellations, such as the Southern Cross. He wondered what life would be like in places like that. But then he realized he'd be doing well just to hold his job here in Waterville Village. It was better than farming. For all the talk about how essential farming was, it didn't bring in much money. Better than working in a store in Newport. That didn't pay much.

For his job you had to have some sense. You had to have a high school education, at least. Ansel swore to himself he would send Jody to college if he could. It was a bad thing to grow up ignorant, like Willis. It made you mean and vicious and hateful. He wouldn't wish that on anybody. He had heard Turner once talking about the Greek philosopher Plato. He had said that Plato said that all evil was really ignorance, and that goodness was knowledge. That made some sense to Ansel. Willis was mean because his vision was clouded and limited by an ignorance about what a good life could be like. Ansel almost felt sorry for him. But not quite. He realized that he might have to kill Willis to protect his family and himself.

As he reached the halfway point on the steps where there was a little sidewalk that broke up the seemingly endless staircase of steps, Ansel saw a familiar figure sitting on the steps above him.

"Hello, Pete," Ansel said. "What you doing up this time of the night?"

"Evening, Ansel," Pete said. "I just came to give you some advice. You know I can't control my brother and what he does. He's swore to kill you for turning him in to Calloway. If I was you I'd leave these mountains and never come back until Willis is dead. That's good advice I'm giving you, Ansel. You can take it or leave it. But when Willis gets a grudge against somebody, he's like a dog with a bone. He won't turn loose 'til you're dead, Ansel. I know him. I ought to. He's my brother."

"I'm not one to run off, Pete."

"Yeah, but you got a nice family to worry about. A nice wife and son, a nice house and a good job. Willis don't have anything very nice. He's got a hell of a lot less to lose than you do."

"You've bailed him out of a lot of scrapes, Pete."

"Yeah, and I guess I always will. He's my brother, Ansel. I just wanted to warn you. Take your family and get out of here. Maybe you could have the company transfer you over toward Asheville. Maybe that'd be far enough away so that Willis would forget you. He'll play with you awhile like a cat does a mouse. But he'll kill you and hurt your family."

He got up and dusted off the seat of his pants and walked off down the steps into the darkness.

"See you, Ansel."

"So long, Pete," Ansel answered. He walked wearily up the rest of the steps, past the balsams, to his house.

A cool October wind moved the leaves of the trees, and the squirrels gathered acorns from beneath the great oaks.

CHAPTER SIXTEEN

"Did you have a good night, sweetheart?" Alice asked as she heard Ansel come in the front door. She turned and gasped as he came into the kitchen.

"Not really," Ansel said. His face was bloody all over from the cut above his eye. His mouth was purple and swollen.

"Oh, my Lord," Alice said. She grabbed a washcloth and wet it while Ansel sat down at the table. "Willis again?"

"Yes. He tried to kill me with his bare hands. He'd have shot me if it hadn't been for Turner. I gave him some trouble this time, though."

Alice washed the blood off his face. He took his shirt off and looked at the place on his chest where Willis had kicked him.

"Goodness!" Alice said. "He really did try to kill you. Did he have his gun?"

"Yes, but Turner came out with a shotgun. He made Willis lay his gun down while we fought."

"How long did you fight? It's nearly one o'clock."

"About thirty minutes, I'd guess. I'm worn out."

"How did it end?" Alice asked as she rubbed Ansel's shoulder.

"Willis got up and staggered to his truck. If he hadn't been drunk he would have whipped me and thrown me into the tailrace. We fought all over the parking lot. If he hadn't left I guess I would have tried to throw him over, too."

"It sounds like a real bad fight."

"It was the worst I've ever had. And next time, I'm afraid, he'll be sober."

Jody came into the living room. "What's the matter, Daddy?" he asked.

"Your daddy got into another fight, Jody."

"With Willis?" Jody asked.

"Yes, son. Now go back to bed," Ansel said.

Jody obeyed reluctantly. When he lay down on the bed he took his pillow and hit it once. "That's for you, Willis Broom," he said.

Ansel and Alice went to bed. But Alice couldn't go to sleep. She tossed for a while, then she reached over and shook Ansel awake. "Ansel! Ansel! We've got to talk."

He wiped the sleep out of his eyes and sat up. "What about?"

"We've got to leave here, Ansel."

"That's what Pete Broom was telling me tonight. I can't run, sweetheart. I'd go through the rest of my life with my head down. Would you want that? A husband who tiptoes around, afraid of every shadow?"

"You're a man, Ansel. I know it and you know it. That's all that matters, ain't it? You don't have to prove anything to me."

"I'd like to leave here, too. But if I leave before I've settled with Willis, I'll be leaving here a coward, Alice. Don't you see that?"

"But you don't even have the law on your side, Ansel. You know what Pete said. He'll be on Willis's side all the way."

"I remember when I was a kid there was a bigger kid who pushed everybody around. He finally got to me. He noticed me. If he'd never noticed me, I would have got along fine. He started pushing me around. Every day after school – I was in the fourth grade – he would catch me on the way home and box my ears. And I would run home in tears.

"Then one day my dad set me down when I got home and explained something to me. He said I'd have to do one of two things: either I'd have to whip that bully's ass or take a different way home.

"I took a different way home, but the bully -- his name was Henry – found it out and caught me again anyway. So I fought. I had to. I fought and fought 'til I was bloody and exhausted. But Henry was bloody and exhausted, too. He was really too fat to fight very well, anyway. He finally left me alone. While I was fighting him I decided that I would whip him or die. He didn't have the same kind of resolution. It made the difference."

"But in Willis's case you're going to have to kill him. Can you do that?"

"Maybe I won't have to. Maybe I can figure something out."

"What?"

"I don't know."

"Please, Ansel. Ask Kelly for a transfer to Asheville. They need dispatchers all over North Carolina. You could probably get one right away. And Calloway knows about your trouble with Willis. He'd put in a good word for you. We could be gone by January, Ansel. Please."

"I'll ask for a transfer. But this thing with Willis will come to a head long before that. He's going to try something within a week, I can feel it. I know it. I'll have to do something, but I don't know what. I should have shot him tonight, I guess, or let him fall into the tailrace."

"Then the law would be after you. You can't just shoot a man down, Ansel."

"Yeah. Unless you're Willis Broom."

"Let's try to get some sleep now, Ansel," Alice said. She cut off the bedroom light, and late in the night they went to sleep.

Willis was driving home along the road to Red Dog. Willis was trying to think, to figure out a way to get even with Ansel that would do Ansel justice. He never counted on Ansel being such a fighter. He would have shot Ansel tonight if Turner hadn't come out with that shotgun. Some time I'll get even with Turner, too. But that can wait.

The kid. They've got that kid. If I could get my hands on him Ansel would come after me, and he'd come with a gun. I could shoot him then and Pete would get me out of it.

If I could somehow get into his house. Or in the woods behind his house. He could watch me torture the wife and kid some, Willis thought. I'll figure out something. Something smart.

Willis relished thinking of all the bad things he could do to Ansel and his family. He had to figure it out just right, though, so Pete can get me out of it easy.

Ansel will be mighty sorry he got on my wrong side, Willis thought.

When he got to his house at Red Dog and drove up in the driveway, he could see that the front door was closed and there was no light on in the living room. Carolyn's still gone, he thought, leaving me right when I need her the most. I'll whip her tail when she does come back. And she'll be back, all right. He opened the door and turned on the living room light. He went to the refrigerator to get a beer and when he opened the door a stench met his nostrils and caused him to back away. It smelled like something dead. He picked up a milk bottle and brought it to his nose. It was soured. And there was a slab of beef wrapped in white butcher's paper which had putrified. The refrigerator was warm inside. He grabbed a warm beer.

Goddamn, he thought. She'll regret this. He threw the spoiled milk out the kitchen door and walked back into the living room and turned on the radio. Patsy Cline was singing "Walking After Midnight."

The trees hovered around the little schoolhouse in Mt. Sterling and they sensed the monster Broom drive his truck up to his house. They knew the woman Carolyn was not there, and they felt glad; and they could hear Broom curse and break things in the house.

CHAPTER SEVENTEEN

Carolyn Broom's knees hurt but she felt good. Her folks' floors hadn't been scrubbed so well in years. They were the same old hardwood and linoleum floors she had played on as a child.

She didn't remember a great deal about her childhood. She remembered that she always had chores: mopping, milking, cooking, bringing water from the spring, and on and on.

She looked from the kitchen into the living room where her parents sat listening to the "Obituary Column of the Air," from WCCF in Newport. Every day the Gaston Funeral Home sponsored a listing of the recently dead in the vicinity of Newport, and Mr. and Mrs. Frady were devoted listeners. Organ music played as the announcer read the names.

Carolyn finished up the kitchen floor so that the worn linoleum shone and then she got up and wiped the sweat from her face and came into the living room.

"Want me to fix us something to eat?" she asked.

"Hush!" her mother said, listening to the names of the dead.

"Don't worry, Momma," Carolyn said. "Your name ain't on that list today."

"Hush!" her father said.

Carolyn sat down on the cheap threadbare couch. The announcer droned out the statistics as the organ played a slow version of "The Old Rugged Cross." She looked at her father, remembering what a handsome man he used to be. Her mother was never a pretty woman and never showed any sweetness to anyone.

That was maybe part of the reason her father had always acted in that stupid way he had, always hugging and kissing young women, always flirting. He still did it. She hated him when he acted that way.

She hated him because it reminded her of what he had done to her and her two sisters when they were girls. She had been fourteen.

She had told Marva, who had been sixteen at the time. Marva cried and told her he had done the same thing to her, plenty of times, and to Glen Ellen, too. Glen Ellen was only twelve. Glen Ellen got pregnant by him when she was fourteen and their mama finally had to admit what was going on and confront him with it. It stopped then, but the flirting continued. It was as if he had to make a fool of himself some way or another.

Maybe it was partly their mama's fault, Carolyn thought as she watched her sitting in rapt attention before the radio. She was a woman who seemed to hate having fun.

That was one thing she almost liked about Willis. Screwing for him was fun. But it was all his fun, not hers.

She didn't hate her father. People did worse things to their kids. She had heard stories of the woman in the mountains known as Nance Dude, who left her grandbaby in a rock cliff to die of exposure and starvation. At least James and Ruth Frady had always fed and clothed them.

She didn't hate either of them. She just felt a sharp sense of disgust, a revulsion mixed with loss and regret.

"What'd you say, Carolyn?" her father asked now that the obituaries were over.

"What do you want for supper tonight?" Carolyn asked.

"Make us a bowl of gravy, honey, to go with that smoked ham we got on the back porch."

"And what else?"

"Some of those canned peas would be good. Have we got any, Maw?"

Mrs. Frady said, "Joyce Singletary's husband died, James. I'm sure that was him. Harold Singletary, it said, seventy, of Blossom. That's him. And he died of a long illness, it said."

"Cancer, most likely. Seems like that's all people die of any more," James said.

"We don't have no canned peas," Ruth said.

"We'll eat some of them greasy cutshort beans your mama canned last fall," James decided. "Them 's good."

"Yeah, them are good," Ruth repeated, still sitting in her rocker, waiting for Carolyn to get up and do it. "It's awful nice to have you home for awhile, Carolyn. Me and your daddy's getting old now. I'm sixty-three and he's sixty-eight, and we don't have no help. Glen Ellen's gone off out to Missouri with that salesman she married and Marva's living with that family in Asheville."

"You know," James said, "I'll bet she works like a pure dog for them people. And us with nobody to help us out in our old age."

Carolyn had tired of hearing them talk this way. They had kept it up ever since she got home. They seemed so selfish and babyish in their old age. She got up and walked out to the back porch and got the big piece of ham down from the hook on the wall and cut three thick slices and then a fourth one, for no good reason. She reached up on the shelf in the pantry and got down a big quart jar of beans and then opened the ice-box door and took out a head of lettuce. Then she took all the stuff to the kitchen and lit the cook stove.

She took a pan out to the spring and put water into it and then brought it back and poured some beans into it, enough for three or four people, and set it on the stove. She put a spoonful of lard into a black frying pan and let it melt and then put the four pieces of ham in.

They would want biscuits, she knew, so she took out a big black pan and set it on the table and then took a big old ceramic bowl from the kitchen cabinet and poured some flour into it and some lard and then some milk. She stirred up her batter and as she worked she wondered what Willis was doing. Probably working at the still, she thought, or out getting drunk with Ray and Jeff. She knew the truth. Willis was mean. He has killed people. And he is going to kill Ansel Harper. He is a crazy, mean person, and she hoped never to see him again.

Then she remembered the whiskey money.

Suddenly she realized what she had to do. She had to leave there so Willis could never find her. She would go tomorrow and use some of the money to buy a bus ticket to Missouri to see Glen Ellen and her family. And never come back.

Carolyn felt an urgency to leave Newport before Willis could find her. The trees seemed to whisper, "Hurry! Hurry!"

CHAPTER EIGHTEEN

Ansel woke up early in the morning. Alice and Jody were still asleep. He decided he would make breakfast for them for a change. Alice didn't have to work – that is, go to a job – but her housework really kept her busy, so he thought he'd lighten her burden a bit. He fixed pancakes and bacon and did a passable job.

He nuzzled Alice's ear and she opened her eyes as he opened the shade of the bedroom window.

"What time is it?" she asked.

"It's eight o'clock. Breakfast is ready."

"Mm. It smells good. Pancakes?"

"And bacon. Come on and get up."

"Go get Jody up. He loves pancakes and syrup."

He went into Jody's room. He noticed how Jody looked more like his mother when he was sleeping and more like him when he was awake.

"Get up, partner," Ansel said.

They all three sat down to breakfast. Jody said the blessing and they started eating.

"Have you thought any more about what we talked about last night?" Alice said to Ansel.

Ansel realized he still hurt from the fight with Willis. "No. I still think that no matter whether I get a transfer or not, I'm still going to have to settle up with Willis. It's just a question of whether I should wait for him to make the next move or whether I should take the initiative and go after him."

"How would you go after him? What would you do?"

"Maybe go to his house and call him out."

"What? You'd take your gun and ask him to draw? Like in the Old West?"

"It does sound dumb, doesn't it?"

"We should just leave," Alice said. "Or you need to sneak up on him somehow."

"I can't just murder him. His brother's the sheriff, you know. They'd put me in jail for forty years."

Alice began to cry.

"It'll work out right," Ansel said.

Jody was listening to all this. He knew they were talking about Willis Broom, and he knew they were serious. "Get him to draw, Daddy!" he said. "You can out-draw him. He's big and slow."

"This ain't Dodge City, Jody," Ansel said. "That stuff is just in the movies. It's not real. At least I used to think that."

"But Daddy! Gene Autry would out-draw him! It would be over in a minute and he'd be lying in Boot Hill."

"That's enough, Jody. Go out and play with Duffy and let your Daddy and me talk."

Jody went outside. Duffy came to him grinning a doggy grin. Jody patted her head and sat down on the dead October grass and thought. Why couldn't Daddy out-draw Willis? The bad guy is always slower than the good guy. He remembered the movie last weekend when Gene beat up five or six bad guys all at one time. Daddy's not Gene Autry, though, Jody admitted to himself. And Gene Autry is just in the movies. The stuff he does can't happen in real life.

Jody thought he heard something in the woods. He peered deep into the green shadows of balsam and pine but there was nothing there, only trees and undergrowth. He felt a little afraid. What if Willis killed Daddy? It was an awful thought. He wanted to do something to help, but he didn't know what.

The woods leaned toward Jody and silently wished him well. They wished they could help the little Harper family.

CHAPTER NINETEEN

Alice was pulling on her prettiest dress, the "Alice blue gown," the dress her Mama had made for her. Ansel came into the bedroom.

"Jody's playing. We've got a few minutes," Ansel said, putting his arms around her waist from behind.

"No," she said, pulling away. "We'd better go on. I told Mrs. Cooper we'd have Jody there about six. You can wait until after the dance."

"Okay," Ansel said resignedly. "You look real pretty."

Sarah Bryson came out of the bathroom, wiping her face with a towel on which she had run cold water from the tap. She had vomited over and over until she had dry heaves. Now she was spent. The children were outside.

She picked up one of the twenties, from the coffee table. It had lipstick in the pattern of a woman's lips across Jackson's picture. It was the one she had kissed when Johnny had brought it home. She had kissed it because it had represented her new winter coat, the white artificial fur one, she had seen in the window of Sellar's Department Store in Newport.

It was the money Willis took from Johnny. But what could she do? How did Pete get hold of it?

She put her head in her hands and cried softly. She got up and went to the phone and dialed a number.

"Hello," her father answered.

"It's me, Daddy. I'm coming to stay with you."

The old man said, "That's good news, Sarah. Good news."

"Do you want me to come and get you?"

"I've got Johnny's car. I'll drive it."

"Be careful, Sarah. I need you."

"I need you, too. Think you can put up with three kids?"

"Sure. Come on."

"I'll be there in an hour or so."

On the way to the dance Alice asked, "How did a hoodlum like Pete Broom get to be sheriff of Haywood County, anyway?"

"He used to work for Jake McConnell and Prentice Hall. He still does, really. They are deep into shady deals. Pete makes it easy for them to operate in Haywood County."

"But why do the people stand for it? Why don't they vote him out?"

"You remember last election when Dave Rinehart ran against him? Pete and two of his deputies whipped him and then put him in jail for being drunk and disorderly. People are afraid to run against him. The main thing is he's got people buffaloed. Which makes him a pretty good sheriff, for little stuff. And little stuff is most of the job."

"But he's corrupt."

"People vote for him anyway. They figure nobody's perfect."

"It's a shame," Alice said. "It's just one more reason for us to get out of here, Ansel."

"There's corruption everywhere, Alice. Not just here."

"Let's talk about something nice, Ansel. Let's have a good time tonight, in spite of everything."

"Okay. That sounds good to me. No more talk about Willis and Pete."

✳ ✳ ✳

The forest watched the humans' dances. The humans would drink too much and fight one another, and then they would drive their cars crazily and often wreck and kill themselves, and start awful fires and cause fearsome explosions. They seemed so blessed in so many ways but could not appreciate it.

The old pine tree quoted further:

"I am weary of your quarrels,
Weary of your wars and bloodshed,
Weary of your prayers for vengeance."

CHAPTER TWENTY

The dance at the Casa Grande was not yet in full swing when Ansel and Alice pulled into the parking lot. The dust raised by the cars on the dirt road outside the dance hall settled on Alice's dress.

When they got to the Casa Grande it was after sundown, but they could see a gathering of men in the back yard of the dance hall. Several men stood in a circle with flashlights pointed at the center.

"What are they doing, Ansel?" Alice asked.

"It's a cockfight. They gamble on it. Whoever's rooster lives is the winner."

"That ought to be against the law," Alice said. "It's so cruel."

"It is. But they do it anyway."

"It seems like the law isn't good for anything."

"People would be much worse, than they are if it weren't for the law, sweetheart."

"I guess you're right. Wait a minute." She picked a long white thread off Ansel's blue coat. "Okay. Now let's go in," she said, smiling up at him.

The dance hall was dimly lit, with a Mexican motif. The waitresses had red skirts and white blouses and the waiters had black pants and white shirts and black cummerbunds, to look like bullfighters.

"Sit at this table and I'll get us a drink. What do you want?"

"You pick me out something, not too strong."

In a few minutes he came back carrying two large drinks. "It's the specialty of the house," he said. "Margueritas."

Alice tasted hers. "It's good. What's this crust around the top? It tastes like salt."

"It is. The drink's got tequila and lime juice in it. I asked the bartender."

They sat sipping their drinks and looking around for familiar faces. They saw Turner and his wife, Evelyn. They were dancing to a fox trot, although Alice didn't know what a fox trot was.

"Let's dance, Ansel," Alice said, moving in her chair to the music.

"Let's finish our drinks first. Then we won't care whether we can dance or not. What kind of dance is that, anyway?"

"I don't know what it's called. See how graceful they look? This is so nice, Ansel. Thank you for bringing me. I'm having such a good time."

"Glad to oblige. I just wish I knew how to dance better."

"You'll do all right. Watch Turner."

Turner and Evelyn twirled about on the dance floor, like spinning tops. Ansel watched him enviously. He must have learned stuff like that in college, he thought. Deep down it looked queer to him. He sipped slowly on his drink.

The next dance was a waltz. He could approximate that, so he took Alice's hand and they joined the other dancers.

When the slow dance was over Ansel and Alice went back to their table. Turner saw them and smiled broadly. "Hey, Ansel, over here!" he said loudly.

Ansel and Alice were embarrassed, but they got their drinks and made a sign to the waitress that they were moving.

"Out on the town, huh?" Turner said, grinning. "The waitresses take orders for dinner. I hear the steaks are good. Have you had dinner?"

"We ate before we left home," Ansel said. Alice sat quietly. She always felt dumb around Turner because he was always quoting poems and such and showing off his college education.

"Someday they'll dig up Newport, Ansel, and some archeologist will marvel to find this place, with all its Mexican artifacts. They'll wonder what century to put it in. Are you enjoying yourselves?"

"Sure are. And listen, Turner, I want to thank you again ...".

"Forget it. You'd have done the same for me. Willis is a coward, really. All bullies are. Say, that's "Maria Elana." It's a tango! Let's go, Alice."

"I don't know how to tango, Turner," she said, blushing and looking down at her cheap red shoes. She looked in horror at the buckle on the left one. It had broken loose and was hanging from the shoe.

"I'll show you how. Just follow me and do what I do, okay?" He grabbed her hand and pulled her up and walked her out onto the dance floor with four other couples.

"Isn't that a great band? They can play anything," Turner said. He smelled nice and Alice tried to relax and follow him and forget about the hanging buckle. Turner walked her backward a few steps and bent her over backwards and laughed and pulled her up again. She felt she was getting the hang of it and suddenly her right foot fell upon the dangling buckle and she pitched forward into Turner's arms.

"Umm," he said, not missing a beat. "Your hair smells so nice. What is that? I'll get Evelyn some."

"It's Toni," she said. "And Avon."

"Avon? Really?" Turner laughed.

"What's funny about Avon?" She was offended.

"Nothing," Turner said, turning red under his tan. "I just didn't realize Avon stuff smelled so good. Maybe it's because it's on you."

She smiled at his effort to patch things up. Then she stepped on her buckle again and sat down in the floor.

"What's wrong?" Ansel asked. "The song's not over."

"It's these damn cheap shoes," she said. "The buckle's come loose."

She turned in her chair and stuck out her foot and Ansel pulled out his pocket knife and opened it and reached down and grabbed her shoe and sliced the buckle off. "There," he said. "That fixes that."

"If it doesn't fall off," she said doubtfully, kicking her foot up and down.

Turner came back through the crowd of dancers. "Trouble with your shoes? Did you hurt yourself?"

"I'm okay. Ansel fixed it. Maybe I'd better stick to the slow dances."

"You were fine. We'll try it again, okay?"

"Not tonight," Alice said, finally. The band started playing "Alice Blue Gown." Alice looked at Ansel in surprise and pleasure. Ansel got up and led her back out on the floor.

"Keep it slow, Ansel," she said, "or I'll fall on my ass again."

"Sure," Ansel said, pulling her close to him.

A thought popped into her mind. "Ansel, did you ask them to play that?"

"Who, me?" Ansel replied, grinning and looking past her.

"You did. I know you did. You're so sweet, Ansel. I love you so much."

"I love you, too," he said. "And I thought it would make you feel better after you showed your ass." They both laughed. When the song was over they came back to the table and sat down.

"How about going outside for a smoke, Ansel?" Turner said. "It's so hot in here."

"Okay. Will you girls be okay while we're gone? Don't get picked up." Alice and Evelyn giggled girlishly, as they were expected to do.

"Nice to get away from the kids for a change, huh, Ansel?" Turner said when they were outside. "The girls need it."

"What made you come out tonight, too?" Ansel asked, genuinely curious.

"We come out every Saturday night. So it's not as big a coincidence as you might think."

"I hear it gets rough," Ansel said.

"Late on Saturday night it often does. The city police show up at eleven. It's just nine now. The night is young."

Ansel inhaled his Camel and looked up through the oak trees at the pale moon. A breeze ruftled his white shirt. He took his coat off and let it cool him.

"Carolina Moon," Turner said. "If we were in Carolina and not Tennessee. The last song they play, right before midnight, is 'Tennessee Waltz'."

Ansel watched the parking lot. A green pickup truck had just pulled in. Two men got out, loud and completely drunk, and staggered toward the entrance of the Casa Grande, where Ansel and Turner stood.

"It's Willis and Ray," Turner said. "Let's get back inside. The manager won't let them in."

They threw their cigarettes away into the boxwoods beside the walk that led up to the entrance and ducked back inside and went over to the table where their wives were waiting and sat down.

"Here they come," Evelyn said confidentially, touching Alice's arm. They had been talking about Ansel's transfer.

"Some little secret, girls?" Turner asked.

"Never you mind," Evelyn said, reaching over to kiss him on the cheek. "This song's about over and I want to dance the next one with Ansel. Whether it's slow or fast. Okay, Ansel?" she asked, smiling charmingly.

"You're on," Ansel said. "Whether I can dance it or not."

The next song was "South of the Border," played western style. A tan and handsome young man in a white dinner jacket sang it at the microphone *a' la* Gene Autry. It came out more like a tango than anything else and so Evelyn was put in the position of teaching Ansel to tango.

She pulled him forward a few steps and pushed him back and then she would hold on to his jacket for dear life and dip down toward the floor. The music was almost done when something struck Ansel's shoulder and spun him around, hard.

It was Willis Broom.

The great forest heard the dance music and the trees swayed and whispered the song the humans were playing: "Tennessee Waltz." The humans seemed to be happy.

CHAPTER TWENTY-ONE

Ray and Willis stood grinning drunkenly at Ansel. Ansel looked around the room. The music went on to the end but the dancers had stopped and backed away from the three men. Out of the corner of his eye Ansel saw Bob and Patricia Kelly and Will and Sylvia Mundy. He wondered what they were all doing here in the Casa Grande.

"Hello, Ansel," Willis said gruffly.

"Hello, Willis," Ansel replied, positioning his weight over the balls of his feet and stooping a little to lower his center of gravity. He had learned that in CCC.

"We got a score to settle, Ansel," Willis said, still grinning. "But not tonight. You go ahead and have a nice time tonight. Where's the kid? Jody?"

"He's with a baby sitter, Willis. Why do you want to know?" Ansel felt a sick feeling crawl up from his belly.

"Are you sure? You real sure he's where you left him? With old Mrs. Cooper?"

Ansel turned white and kept looking at Willis and Ray. Ray had a match stem in his mouth and one of his upper front teeth was gone.

"Maybe you best check on him, Ansel. Maybe he ran off or something."

"Willis, if you mess with my family, I'll kill you."

"Whoo! Big talk from the little man," Ray said, and both he and Willis laughed.

The music started up again. It was "Let Me Call You Sweetheart," played in waltz time, and the vocalist sang. A few couples started dancing again.

Turner came up behind Ansel. "Trouble?" he asked.

"Not yet. These two told me I'd better check on Jody."

"You can use the telephone in the office. I'll stay with the girls."

Willis and Ray looked at each other and laughed noisily. Turner went back to the table. Alice and Evelyn were scared.

"What's the matter?" Alice asked.

"They made some crack about Jody. Ansel's calling Mrs. Cooper now. Don't be upset. Willis is just bluffing, trying to spoil our evening. Don't worry about it. Let's dance."

"Not right now. I don't feel like it," Alice said.

"Look, Alice!" Is that Bob Kelly? And isn't that Sylvia Mundy he's dancing with? And Will is dancing with Patricia."

Alice was too worried to hear Evelyn. She was watching the office door where Ansel had just entered. Finally he came out and came back to the table. He met Alice's worried look with reassurance. "He's okay. Mrs. Cooper put him to bed an hour ago."

"So let's dance," Turner said, grabbing Alice's hand. She got up and went with him to the center of the floor just as the music stopped. They laughed together as they waited for the next song.

"The band gets a little wild around this time," Turner warned. And sure enough, when the band started up again, it was with "Orange Blossom Special."

"I can't dance to that, Turner. Let's sit down," Alice said.

"It's a square dance, Alice. Somebody will start calling in a minute. You can square dance, can't you?"

"Well, some," Alice grinned.

Someone, a man, called out "Eeyaa-haa," and the dancers knew he would be the caller. They danced as couples until he cried "Circle!" and the couples, of which there were six, moved into a circle. "Dosee-do," the caller shouted, and the dancers gathered up in a bunch.

Suddenly Turner was no longer at Alice's side. She looked around and Ray was marching him out the door, one hand gripping his collar and the other the seat of his pants. Willis was leaned against the bar gulping down a beer and grinning.

"Stop," Evelyn shouted, and ran out the door behind the two men. Some of the dancers looked but continued with the square dance. Alice looked around to find Ansel and saw him coming through the crowd of dancers, a grim look on his face.

"Wait, Ansel," she said. "Don't go out there."

"I have to, Alice. It's because of me he's in trouble now. I've got to go." He walked swiftly through the front door and out into the parking lot.

Alice watched Willis. He finished his beer and ordered another and drank that down without taking it from his lips, his Adam's apple jumping up and down. Then he strode carelessly toward the front door. Alice followed him out the door and as Willis walked across the parking lot toward the others she hid in the shadows of the doorway, watching. She thought of the P.38 in the glove compartment of their Chevrolet and wondered whether, if she ran, she could get to it in time.

Ray was punching Turner in the face. Turner's glasses lay broken on the gravel. Evelyn was standing by, shouting "Hit him, Ralph, hit him!" but this wasn't helping at all. Ray continued to pound at him mercilessly and Turner continued to stand and take it.

Ansel took dead aim from ten feet and ran at Ray as hard as he could. He caught Ray in the lower back and knocked him five feet. Both men fell together, and Turner turned and staggered and fell in a senseless heap. Evelyn ran to him and shook him.

"Ralph! Get up! Please," she begged, but Turner was unconscious. "Please, someone call the sheriff! They're beating my husband to death."

Ansel wound up on top of Ray and started punching him in the face. He felt some teeth give and then he felt the nose cartilage give way. Ray yelled out but Ansel continued punching him.

Ansel looked around to see what had become of Willis and at that moment Willis's shoe came up into his belly, lifting him off Ray and dumping him on his face. Ansel couldn't breathe, he couldn't cry out. He felt as if he were dying. He blacked out and lay still. Alice screamed and ran out of the shadows as she saw Willis walk over to the unconscious Ansel.

"Stop, stop, please," she cried out. Willis looked around, still grinning.

Willis grabbed her arm as she ran past him.

"What do you want, you bastard?" Alice asked, crying. He shook her and laughed. Then he looked down to see if Ansel was conscious. He was coming to, groaning and sucking in his breath.

"Look here, Ansel," Willis said, and pulled Alice to him.

"Oh, God," Alice screamed.

"Willis!" A voice boomed across the parking lot. Willis turned around. The beam of a flashlight hit his eyes, blinding him momentarily.

"Willis Broom, is that you?" the voice asked.

"It's me. Who the hell are you?"

"Sheriff Lane Moss, of Cocke County, Tennessee, at your service, Mr. Broom. You people are under arrest for disturbing the peace and public drunkenness."

"You got to prove that, sheriff. I ain't drunk. Maybe these fellows here are, but I ain't. I only had two beers."

"I know you, Willis. And I know that fat, worthless brother of yours, too. You think you're beyond the law. Well, you ain't. All of you better get into your cars and go home. We don't put up with shit like you in Cocke County."

"Yes, sir, sheriff. We're leaving right now," Willis said in his squeaky voice. "Let me get my friend up and I'll drive him home right now."

The doctor looked Turner over. Turner's eyes were swollen and one of his upper front teeth had been knocked out.

The doctor felt his ribs and listened to his chest. "He's had a bad beating. We'll need to keep him at the clinic a few days. He'll be bruised badly. He might have a broken rib."

If undisturbed by storms or power-saws, trees could live for hundreds of years, years of peace. It saddened them to see the awful beating the friend of Ansel had received. They whispered to one another about the monster Broom, and hoped he would quickly die, as so many such people often did. Hatred and fear grow, and Willis had done such hateful, fearsome things.

CHAPTER TWENTY-TWO

Willis went around to the Harper's back door. He knew he would have to do this job by himself.

He pushed on the screen door gently and it was not latched. Then he turned the knob of the wooden door and it was locked. He took the crowbar and slipped the bent end between the door lock and the door and gently, gently prized the door open.

Alice had the radio on, listening to "Suspense" and Jody was asleep on the couch with Duffy snoozing beside him.

When Willis proceeded into the living room Duffy perked up her ears and when she saw Willis she started barking furiously, waking Jody and rousing Alice from her radio program.

Willis jumped to the couch and grabbed up Jody around the waist. Then he kicked Duffy as hard as he could and the dog ran away, whimpering and hopping.

"Ansel don't get home 'til about 12:15," he said in his squeaky voice. "We can have some fun before that, huh?"

"Please, Willis," Alice said, crying. "Don't hurt us."

"Call the plant and tell Ansel I'm here for a little visit. Tell him not to bring nobody else, nor no gun, or I'll finish you and the kid off."

She did as she was told. Ansel left the plant on a run. By the time he got to the house he was exhausted. The porch light was on, as it always was when he came home at night.

Ansel had not followed all of Willis's directions. He had his P.38 in the pocket of his coat.

He saw Willis through the front window. He had Jody around the waist and was sitting with him on the couch. Alice was standing against the wall beside the kitchen.

Ansel kicked in the front door and aimed his P.38 at Willis but Willis was too quick and shot Ansel and then aimed again, but this time Alice had grabbed a butcher knife from the kitchen and stuck it into Willis's back.

Ansel fell unconscious at Willis's feet. Jody had grabbed Ansel's P.38 and was pointing it at Willis.

Willis ducked out the broken front door and ran down the steps and down the sidewalk to the plant parking lot and got in his truck and drove away.

Willis leaned back in his seat and discovered the knife was still there, so he stopped and pulled it out and it bled terribly. He drove to Red Dog and went inside and found a towel to stanch the flow.

The money, he thought. He had almost forgotten it. He knew very well Pete had it.

The trees could sense what had happened in the Harper house. How long would this monster Broom survive, the trees murmured to one another. "Somehow we must do something," one large old tree said. It was a maple. It had one broken limb that was hanging over Willis's still.

CHAPTER TWENTY-THREE

When Pete learned of Willis's assault on the Harpers he knew he would have to arrest Willis. He took Deputy Lamarr along.

"You go around the left side of the house," Pete told Lamarr, "and I'll go around the right side. Willis will be at his still. He's hurt and he's mad as hell. So watch yourself. I'll go up to the still from the front and you go around the still through the woods and come up on him from behind that big maple tree."

"Okay," Deputy Lamarr said.

They both pulled their guns and crept around the house and up toward the still.

Pete stepped out into the small clearing. Willis was sitting on a river rock beside the big maple tree. He had his .38 in his hand. He had heard the patrol car drive up.

"Hello, little brother," Pete said.

"Where is my money, Pete?" Willis asked.

"I ain't got it," Pete said.

"Lying bastard," Willis said.

"That's not my reason for being here, Willis," Pete said. "I'm here to arrest you for shooting Ansel Harper. He's in Haywood County Hospital. He might die. And you terrorized Alice and little Jody. I got to take you in."

Deputy Lamarr stepped forward, crushing some dry leaves under his feet, and Willis heard him and swung around and shot at him and he ducked behind the maple tree.

Pete fired at Willis but missed him, and Willis shot Pete in the belly.

Willis heard a loud cracking noise above him and he looked up and a dead branch on the huge maple tree fell. As it fell its branches caught in a smaller tree and the huge limb fell with the split-off part, which made it into a kind of scythe, swung down and caught Willis in the abdomen and lifted him off the ground.

Willis swung a few moments, two feet off the ground, blood spurting out of his abdomen just under his ribs.

His eyes opened and he still had his gun in his hand so Deputy Lamarr shot him over and over until his own gun was empty.

Willis's eyes were set now but the deputy watched him for several moments. The deputy's hand was trembling badly. Then he looked at Pete, who was motionless, lying on his face. He went closer and asked, "Where is the money, Pete?"

But Pete was dead.

"The monster Broom is dead, and his brother, too," the Great Maple said. "Their souls can have no place among us. They must go into the endless darkness, which the humans call Hell."

The trees felt joy.

CHAPTER TWENTY-FOUR

Jody was sitting in the back of the Chevrolet looking out the window. It was a cold and snowy January day. "Howdy Doody" was on the car radio. The Harper family was leaving Waterville Village, behind a Mayflower moving van that crept along in front of them. There was ice on the road up Cataloochee and both van and car were forced to go very slowly, but not <u>too</u> slowly, to avoid sliding off the narrow mountain road into the deep valley below.

"This must be the worst day of the worst winter in years," Ansel said, peering through the snowfall. "Maybe we ought to go back and try again tomorrow."

"No, Ansel. We can make it. I don't want to go back to Waterville Village for anything."

"Are you sorry I couldn't get a transfer to Asheville, where your people live?" Ansel asked.

"No. We shouldn't get right on top of them anyway," Alice replied. "We're lucky they had a vacancy at the substation in Canton."

"It doesn't hurt to have family around," Ansel said. "My family are all in Alabama. They couldn't be much help to me anyway. They're all poor as Job's turkey."

"I'm just glad we're getting out alive. Do you have any regrets about leaving, Ansel?"

"Not a one," Ansel said.

Jody looked out the back window. He had his Gene Autry cowboy outfit on – the hat, the guns, the sweater, the boots, even a Gene Autry watch. He had got it all for Christmas. And he had his coat on over it. He was watching the woods on the left side of the car go by. He was scared to watch the right side. It just dropped off into deep forests. The tops of the trees were even with the road. It was scary.

Suddenly the car started to slide toward the bank, the wheels spinning on the ice. Ansel and Alice and Jody held their breath until the tires caught. Ansel had snow grip tires on, no chains. They let out their breath at the same time. Ansel and Alice laughed.

"I'm glad we're moving out of Waterville Village. I want Jody to have some education. I want him to have a chance in life. People back in Waterville don't have a dog's chance. No offence, Duffy," Alice said.

Duffy was asleep on the back seat beside Jody, but she opened her eyes and looked up when her name was mentioned.

Jody was watching the trees go by as they picked up speed. The ones in front went by quickly and those farther back went by more slowly. He fixed his eyes on a distant maple tree, a big one. The other trees went by in front of it but it seemed to stay in the same place. But soon it, too, was gone.

It had seemed to Jody that this tree had a face, a kind of human face, which almost seemed to smile. The tree seemed to wave one of its limbs to him.

EPILOGUE

The quotes by the old pine tree are from "The Song of Hiawatha," by Henry Wadsworth Longfellow, 1855.

This story is based on true events that happened to real people. The Harpers – Ansel, Alice, and Jody – are based on my father and my mother and me. Willis Broom and most of the other characters were also based on real individuals, but I have changed their names.

The pictures in the book belong to the author.

Waterville, Mt. Sterling, Cataloochee Mountain, Waynesville (all in N.C.), and Newport, TN are real places.

My dad's P.38 was real, and I can still feel the fear I had for Willis Broom. He really carried a Smith & Wesson .38 special.

The power plant is real and so is Walters Dam, and so are the Great Smoky Mountains.

My mother never got to see Paris or Casablanca. My father worked almost 40 years for the power company. My parents were decent, good people. They sent me and my younger brother to college. They sacrificed so much, and I didn't really appreciate them until they were dead. Sometimes I ache with sorrow for them. Sometimes I still can feel the warmth of their love for my younger brother and me.

Sometimes I can still hear the trees whisper; sometimes I can hear them sing!

THE END